265.94
S979e

DETROIT PUBLIC LIBRARY

3 5674 05389390 6

An
Exorcist's
Field Guide

To
Blessings,
Consecrations
and
Banishment of
Malevolent Entities

By Pastor Swope

Open Gate Ministerial Services Publishing

2009

MAY   2015

HUBBARD BRAI
12929 W. Mc
DETROIT, M
313-481-

D1376929

HU

MAY 2014

2

Table of Contents

3

Introduction

This book is not meant to be comprehensive in its reach; it is for the beginner who for one reason or another has been put in the position of confronting a possible demonic or malevolent infestation of a location or the oppression of an individual. It is not a guide to the process of Exorcism of a possessed individual, although some of the principles are the same.

This guide is Christian in its worldview and therefore the Prayers and Invocations therein reflect Traditional Christian Theology and Biblical concepts. Therefore those of other faiths might use this as a starting point for their own rite, but I advise you to seek out a professional in your own belief system.

A warning; dealing with malevolent entities is not casual business. While this guide can give you the basics as how to deal with such beings there comes a time to know your limitations. It could be that the use of this guide might provoke more powerful entities. However, if used with faith and the combined prayer of others this guide should be effective for most situations. If there is an increase of activity or physical manifestations, a professional should be contacted as soon as possible.

Do not confront any malevolent entity alone. Always have a support team with you and at least two others who are devoted to prayer during the encounter.

Definition of commonly used terms:

Entity: An ethereal creature that is perceived to interact with the earthly plane of existence. A spirit, force or sentient being that is not 'physical' in our sense of the word.

Practitioner: The person in control of the spiritual encounter with the entity.

Associate: Those who assist the Practitioner.

Possession: The state in which an entity physically inhabits a host and controls that person's motivations, desires and actions. It is usually accompanied by paranormal manifestations.

Oppression: The state in which an entity harasses an individual physically, psychologically and/or incidentally. In many cases it will 'latch on' to an individual and in extreme cases, begin to influence the person in various ways.

Binding: The action by which the exorcist constricts the activity of the entity through commands empowered with spiritual authority.

Exorcism/Deliverance/Power-Encounter: The action by which the exorcists cleanses a location or person of demonic or malevolent entity infestation through spiritual battle.

Blessing: The action of invoking the favor of God on a place or person.

Consecration: The setting aside of a person or place for the special attention and presence of God. Willful surrender of the place or person for purposeful use by God and His will.

Cleansing: Purging a person or place of a malevolent entity or demonic spirit.

Banishment: Forcing the entity by command to leave the area, abandon its current sphere of influence and dwell in a place of confinement (the abyss).

There are many ways to approach demonic deliverance, and this is only one style. It is in no way fool proof or complete. This style is very clinical and direct, using prayer and commands in the name of Jesus Christ with certain ceremonial accoutrements. Other intercessors use various other rites, procedures or tools. I personally have found this approach to be the most thorough and effective when in comes to minor infestations.

Some prayers, blessings and all scripture will be in both English and Latin. Not for showmanship or novelty, these entities have been around for thousands of years and know Latin as well as English. Personally, I have found that the use of Latin does inspire faith and confidence in some, so I would be remiss to exclude it.

Since I started my blog, The Paranormal Pastor, a week has not gone by in which I have not received a request by an individual or group as to how to proceed in the area of demonic or malicious entity activity.

It is my hope that this guide gives some help to those who have no one to turn to in such situations. It is not an easy task, and to be approached with much caution and spiritual discernment. And it is a task that is definitely not to be taken lightly as entertainment. If you do so you may find yourself in a very bad place, personally.

Proceed with caution,

Pastor Swope

The Rite

Exorcism is a religious rite.

Therefore it is immersed in Theological belief.

This approach centers on The Lord Jesus Christ and His authority and dominion over the cosmos. The power to do this rite does not come from the practitioner; it comes from the authority and Lordship of Christ over these entities.

 Luke 10:18-20 (KJV) *abridged* says: *"And he said unto them, I beheld Satan as lightning fall from heaven. Behold, I give unto you power... over all the power of the enemy: and nothing shall by any means hurt you... the spirits are subject unto you."*

The rite is able to produce results because of the intimate relationship that the practitioner has with Christ in faith.

Faith is the key to success in deliverance.
It is the area that the entity will attack you most vehemently.

Although not specifically addressed in scripture, many who deal with demonic forces notice that they have a certain inroad to the human consciousness. Is it, as some would determine, a form of mental telepathy? Or is it that these ancient beings who have observed and manipulated human beings for untold millennia have a certain knack for knowing the human condition and extrapolating what their thoughts are. Much like we do with those who are emotionally close to us but to an infinitesimal degree.

Whatever the means these creatures are able to play with the human mind and prey upon our greatest fears.

Thus they are able to attack the practitioner at his/her most vulnerable areas and affect a weakening of faith.

They usually do this in three areas: doubt, fear and sin.

These three are interconnected in impact on the human psyche but separate in method of attack.

Doubt: Of course we are mere mortals treading in areas of the unknown. It is natural to feel inadequate in battling these entities. They exploit these innate emotions and use them to their advantage. From a nagging feeling that you are over in your head to outright failure when performing a part of the rite, the entities will try to disable you through disbelief in the effectiveness of the rite or your ability to perform it adequately.

Fear: We all have our pre-conceived notions when it comes to malicious entities. Modern media's interpretation of demonic forces has not helped us form a realistic critical understanding of these supernatural beings.

We often attribute power to them that they do not have.

Likewise we often ignore the powers and abilities they do have to cause harm to the individual because of ignorance or negligence. We often expect the manifestation of the supernatural to have all the bells and whistles we see in modern horror films. Physical manifestations, preternatural abilities and powers of the demonic are intellectual expectations than vary in form and intensity from culture to culture. But many times the real supernatural aspects of a demonic encounter are subtle and devious. Not frightening as they are manipulative.

14

When a demonic presence uses overt dramatic means to frighten the practitioner or his/her associates, its chief motivation is to dishearten and discourage. It wants the rite to be stopped no matter how extreme it must behave. Paranormal incidents such as visual and auditory phenomena along with 'telekinetic' or 'poltergeist like' physical disturbances are means to instill fear and doubt into the heart of the very person the entity fears. It is very rare that such phenomena can actually cause harm to the practitioners despite fictional or scripted 'real life' dramatizations that are currently in vogue among the paranormal community. Such occurrences do take place but they are the rarity and often occur at the site of multiple entity infestations or a site that has long been dedicated to nefarious ceremonies or activities.

For the most part the practitioner or the associates are overcome with the emotion by direct or indirect manipulation of the entity. These feeling are volatile for those in the team who are sensitive emotionally or spiritually. Encouragement through prayer and scripture reading is encouraged and appropriate readings are included in Prayers and Scripture Passage sections.

Sin: In Biblical Theology, mankind is an imperfect creature because of the sin nature. Various branches of Christianity have varying views on the nature of sin and humanity, but all agree that we are flawed and imperfect creatures in need of liberation from our seemingly unlimited ability to do evil to each other for the pettiest reasons. We as Christians have that liberation from our base nature in the sacrifice of Jesus Christ. However we need to accept the forgiveness of Christ and turn away from our sin and confess them. Many clergy call this 'keeping a short list' before God. Of course these are the basics of Christianity and need not be extrapolated upon here. There are a multitude of resources for those seeking

spiritual growth and techniques to break from habitual sin
and lead a life of peace and wholeness.

However, unrepentant or unforgiven sin can be a huge
liability for the practitioner or the associates. There are
spiritual, emotional and psychological aspects to
unforgiven sin, and to become engaged in a spiritual
battle with malevolent forces while weighed down by sin
and guilt can be very hazardous.

Firstly it gives an inroad to the enemy. Malicious entities
can 'latch' onto a person riddled with guilt over their
shortcomings. The entities can exacerbate the personal
problems the individual is facing and make their issues
worse off than they were at the beginning. If there are
addictions involved there could be an uncontrollable
surge of irresponsible behavior, driving the person to the
brink of disaster and mental instability. Often times there
are unnatural desires for other destructive behaviors the

individual has never had issue with previously. Suck 'latching on' by entities are at least oppression and could lead to full blown possession.

Secondly, unconfessed or unrepentant sin disables the internal faith of the practitioner and the associates. There is a constant doubt because you know you are not right before God. God requires a clean vessel to work with when it comes to spiritual battle. Not a prefect vessel, but a vessel that is honest before God about his/her shortcomings and is has made steps to receive forgiveness before God through the blood of Christ. Doubt makes you ineffective because you do not believe you can do the cleansing. Because deep down inside you know that you yourself need a cleansing as well.

Thirdly, if there is a especially powerful entity involved there is a good chance that one way or another it knows of your problems and will be delighted to exploit that personal shortcoming or (although only in rare and extreme circumstances) it can reveal your shortcoming to anyone who cares to hear. It can be an embarrassing and confusing moment of chaos that will actually strengthen the entity and make the situation worse for the very people you were trying to help.

Preparation

Before the encounter the practitioner should choose the associates who will assist and determine what their roles should be. You should not take on the assignment alone; your associates are your lifeline in case you should run into trouble. Associates primary role is to pray, therefore it is essential that those in the role have a cultivated spiritual life of faith. Their support does not have to be in the same physical location that the encounter occurs, but it is recommended. Their presence at the site is necessary if you have any inkling that the entity you will encounter could be active and malevolent. In the best of scenarios you will have associates both praying for your team at another location and also two or three with you while the spiritual battle takes place. Scripture repeatedly says that, "Out of the mouth of two or three witnesses, every word will be established" (Duet 19:15; Matt 18:16; 2 Corinthians 13:1) this is a spiritual principle of unity that is most effective in spiritual battle. Your associates should agree with you in prayer, scripture and commands.

Before entering the location you are to cleanse you and your associates should pray. Pray for protection, wisdom, strength and guidance. Have everyone pray for each other and ask for God's protection. Examples of such prayers will be given in the chapter Introductory Prayers.

It is best that you know all that you can of the situation at hand before you enter the area affected. It is best if this precursory information is attained well in advance, but if it cannot or if there are other issues to be examined before you begin it is best to do so before entering the physical area. This is because you do not want to discuss the proceedings you are about undertake in the possible presence of the entities. It can lead to a more difficult encounter.

Spiritually Sealing the Area

Once you enter the location you should seal it off. That is, through prayers and actions prevent both the entity from leaving and other entities from swarming into the area. Such transference and conglomeration would drastically complicate the encounter. You should think of it as if you were sealing off a suspect in an isolated interrogation room. Preformed properly the entity cannot call or receive help from its own contacts. It is alone and at a disadvantage, and you can proceed with the cleansing without the complication of outside harassment.

Scriptural Reading

The reading of pertinent portions of Scripture proceeding the sealing does two things:

One, if there is a malicious entity in the area sealed off they will become increasingly agitated by the reading of scripture. They cannot escape and the selected Scripture is meant to remind them of their ultimate defeat and hopeless condition. Sometimes they will become so disoriented or agitated that they reveal themselves in a paranormal event. The continued reading will weaken the entity so they can be more readily dealt with in the remainder of the rite.

Two, the reading of self same Scriptures will encourage the practitioner and increase faith. Assenting to the truth of the read word gives the team spiritual power just as much as it drains the demonic force. **Hebrews 14:12** tells us, *"the word of God is quick, and powerful, and sharper than any two edged sword, piercing even to the dividing asunder of soul and spirit, and of the joints and marrow,* *and is a discerner of the thoughts and intents of the*

heart." (KJV)

This mutual assent to the truth binds both the practitioner

and associates to the same goal and mindset when

approaching the potential spiritual battle ahead. We know

that God in Christ is our strength and we rely upon Him

and not to our own devices, which is a critical concept

when dealing with possible malignant entities.

Commands

All entities are obliged to obey commands of authority on

one level or another. The key concept for the effectual use

of commands is *AUTHORITY.*

Webster defines the word authority as someone who has

the legal power to enforce. It is a power or right that has

been given or delegated to the individual. A home owner

and their family has the right to command an entity to

leave. It is their property, their living space which the

entity is trespassing on now, even though they might have staked a claim to it previously. Likewise the exorcist has been given the right through Christ to command any demonic entity. **The Gospel of Mark 16:17** says, ***"And these signs shall follow them that believe; In my name shall they cast out devils..."***

The word translated 'devils' here in the King James Version is the Kione Greek word *Διαμόναι*, which is translated 'demons' in most modern versions of scripture. According to Colin Brown's *Dictionary of New testament Theology*, in popular Hellenistic though 'demon' referred to any entity, and the root word *Δεμόνιον* referred to the god of the dead as the divider of the corpse. It donates superhuman power[1]. There is an ancient tradition that the

---

[1] .Colin Brown, ed., *Dictionary of New Testament Theology Vol. 1* (Exeter,Devon: Pasternoster Press, 1975), 450.

'demon' is the cursed disembodied soul of the offspring of fallen angels and mankind as seen in Genesis 6:1-4, the Nephilim. Rabbinical teachings on demons had many classifications of these beings the most prominent being:

Sedim: Powerful ones, lord demons

Mazzaqim: Harmers

Mehabbelim: Destroyers

Pegaim: Attackers

Ruah ra'ah: Evil spirits

Ruah: Spirit

So within the Theological framework of the New Testament culture this text from the Gospel of Mark tells us that people of faith can cast out these entities by the Name of Jesus Christ of Nazareth.

This is the authority the exorcist has; it has been given to him as a believer in Christ. It is Christ's authority and not our own, for we are but imperfect mortal beings with no power over these creatures. It is by belief in Christ and His redemption and forgiveness that we have the authority over the demonic entity, and any other entity for that matter.

We are imperfect but because of the legal role of the believer as justified in Christ can we have the spiritual authority to cast out the demonic. We may have sinned, but we are not only forgiven but legally declared 'not guilty' in the spiritual realm because of the sacrificial death of Jesus Christ on our behalf.

We are forgiven by His blood by His death, and empowered by His Spirit through His resurrection to cast out the demonic.

And that casting out is done by commands.

That is why when issuing commands we have to make sure we are invoking the Name and the Blood of Jesus Christ of Nazareth.

The Name of Christ is used because of the power and authority that comes from invoking His Name. Just as it is important if at all possible to find out the name of the demonic entity when performing an exorcism when a person is possessed, it is important to use the name of Christ. It is also wise to use the full "In the name of Jesus Christ of Nazareth" or "Jesus Christ the only begotten Son of God" at least once in the cleansing because there has been many instances of demonic entities using the name "Jesus Christ" in general. A rarity, yes, but since many practitioners have run into entities who call themselves thus, it is wise to be specific at least once or twice in the rite.

Invoking the Blood of Christ is done because it is by Christ's blood mankind is saved from hell and through His blood all sins are forgiven. The Blood of Christ is an evocation of cleansing and disempowerment of the hold of evil over a person or place. Through the Blood the place or person is forgiven and the legions of evil are disarmed. The demon has no power when confronted with the Blood of Christ.

The demonic entity has no chance of salvation through the Blood, unlike mankind, and this in effect for a better word 'puts them in their place'. They know they are powerless and eventually doomed for the pit.

When making commands it is best to go from the general to the more specific.
To begin you might say,
"We claim this room in the name of the Lord Jesus Christ"

28

Then later you would move on to a more legal authoritarian stance such as

"In the name and Blood of the Lord Jesus Christ, the only begotten Son of God you are commanded to leave this room and from this time forth you are forbidden to enter its boundaries."

The former being a general command and the later being a more specific claim and command. It is best to start out from the general to the specific because you are in a sense 'teaching' the entity. Some entities are either stubborn or dulled to the material realm so this progression of authoritative commands leaves no room for misunderstanding.

Binding of the spirit

Binding the spirit is a preventative action. It can be done fairly soon in the process and continue on throughout the rite. A binding is a stripping of the spiritual power and influence of the entity in preparation for it being cast out.

29

A binding is a command, but it is more specific. It also is done through the invocation of the Name and Blood of Christ. During the binding it is good to remind the entity that it legally has no power, it must obey. The repetition of a binding in a certain area is up to the practitioner, it may be that he senses there is a spiritual struggle going on or that the command needs to be repeated because of specificity or a paranormal manifestation. A binding is akin to the sealing of the building and room, it is a preventative action to prevent harm from the entity and it also is reinforcement with the sealing to make sure the entity is localized and does not flee.

An very general example would be:

"We bind you in the Name of the Lord Jesus Christ, and by the power of His Blood you are commanded to not to influence anyone or anything in this room."

More specific binding commands will be presented in that chapter itself.

The action of binding comes from the book of **Revelation**

20:1-4

"And I saw an angel come down from heaven, having the key of the bottomless pit and a great chain in his hand. And he laid hold on the dragon, that old serpent, which is the Devil, and Satan, and bound him a thousand years, And cast him into the bottomless pit, and shut him up, and set a seal upon him, that he should deceive the nations no more, till the thousand years should be fulfilled: and after that he must be loosed a little season."

Casting the entity

Casting an entity is to remove it from one location and

sending it to another.

There are two ways to cast an entity. Rather, there are two

places that you can cast an entity. It varies on the

practitioner and their theological background in the realm

of demonology.

One option is to cast the demon into the pit or hell.

Another is to cast it into a location or thing.

31

Casting the entity into the pit is a reflection of the theological assumption that the being is a disembodied spirit of the Nephilim that has escaped the pit of torment where it was to await the final judgment. Those who practice this variation see the importance of making sure the entity can no longer bother anyone else.

Those who prefer to not use this variation say that it a futile gesture since it not only assumes that they have escaped from the pit but more importantly that the pit is not hell but some sort of way station for bound evil beings.

Others would cast the entity into a location or thing. Some older practitioners called this casting the demon into the wilderness.

Now this is literally not a specific location, but an analogy for a place of desolation where it can harm no one. However it references back to a Scriptural passage that curiously would prove otherwise. Jesus says in **Luke 11:24-26**, *"When the unclean spirit is gone out of a man, he walketh through dry places, seeking rest; and finding none, he saith, I will return unto my house whence I came out.*

And when he cometh, he findeth it swept and garnished. Then goeth he, and taketh to him seven other spirits more wicked than himself; and they enter in, and dwell there: and the last state of that man is worse than the first." Some practitioners take this cue from Christ in casting the malevolent entity into the wilderness or the 'dry places' in the King James Version. The Greek term ἀνύδρων τόπων carries the meaning of a lifeless place of desolation. The practitioner would in effect be commanding the demonic entity to go to a place where it can affect no living being.

But as Jesus reports the demonic being finds no rest in the wilderness and soon returns with other entities to reclaim its previous host.

Of course this is a warning that if a person is delivered from a demonic entity they need to be filled with the Holy Spirit in Christ so the entity does not come back and take control once again. Indeed the 'house' would be swept and cleaned during the exorcism but unless it is occupied by the benevolent power of God, the creature and its cohorts will once again inhabit and cause disorder.

In order to avoid this other practitioners follow Jesus' example in **Luke 8:26-33**,

"*And they arrived at the country of the Gadarenes, which is over against Galilee.*

And when he went forth to land, there met him out of the city a certain man, which had devils long time, and ware no clothes, neither abode in any house, but in the tombs.

When he saw Jesus, he cried out, and fell down before him, and with a loud voice said, What have I to do with

34

thee, Jesus, thou Son of God most high? I beseech thee, torment me not.

(For he had commanded the unclean spirit to come out of the man. For oftentimes it had caught him: and he was kept bound with chains and in fetters; and he brake the bands, and was driven of the devil into the wilderness.)

And Jesus asked him, saying, What is thy name? And he said, Legion: because many devils were entered into him.

And they besought him that he would not command them to go out into the deep.

And there was there a herd of many swine feeding on the mountain: and they besought him that he would suffer them to enter into them. And he suffered them.

Then went the devils out of the man, and entered into the swine: and the herd ran violently down a steep place into the lake, and were choked."

But does this do any more good than the other ways? If these entities are eternal spirits then they did not die when the pigs did. It just put them in a place where they could do the victim no more harm for a time.

So no matter the exact formula used , the effect is the same: to remove the entity so the person or place can be cleansed.

Now a;though you will not be using the rituals detailed here for the Exorcism of possessed individuals, the basic rules still apply.

Which brings us to the last part of the rite, which is the **Consecration** .

Simply, the consecration is the inviting of the presence of Christ through the Holy Spirit to dwell and abide in the house. It is done through prayer, Scriptural readings, willful assent by the property's owner or resident and visual aspects of the ritual via Holy Water and sacred incense.

The consecration is done in part throughout the building to be blessed and at the end as a whole for the premises. Scripture readings are to encourage those involved and assert the power of God in the building. The prayers of consecration actively invite the presence and protection of God over the building, which must be in an active consensual agreement with the owner or resident.

The Format for a Custom Ritual

In the following chapters we will use the basic format we just reviewed in a free flowing style so you can customize the ceremony to your needs. Some types of prayers and scriptures will be types that can be interchanged throughout the ritual. These types will be similar in content, effect, and meaning. Using a contemporary illustration of this process, it will be like ordering from a classic Chinese Restraunt You get one from side A, one from Side B and one from side C. Together they form the dinner that is tailored to your need. With this format you are not stuck with one rite, but you can with practice be flexible in accordance with your need. The concluding chapter of this book will give visual examples on how to arrange the ceremony.

Please make yourself familiar with them before you using them in the field.

And many times in this work, flexibility in hand with patience and determination of faith will help one win the day.

Introductory Prayers

Prayer of Cleansing and Empowerment

In the Name of the Lord Jesus Christ, only

begotten Son of God, we ask that Lord Father

you would watch over us tonight and grant that

an army of your angelic host would be at our

side to protect us and assist us in our fight.

We give ourselves to you Lord Jesus and we ask

that your Holy Spirit would guide us, empower

us and help us in the battle this day with the

enemy.

We ask Lord Christ that you would forgive us

any sin we may have committed and not

confessed before you now, in the Blood of our

Savior, the Lord Jesus Christ. Amen

Guardian Angel Prayer (English)

My guardian dear,

To whom his love commits me here;

Ever this (day, night) be at my side,

To light and guard, to rule and guide.

Amen.

(Latin)

qui custos es mei,

Me tibi commissum pietate superna;

(Hodie, Hac nocte)   ecure o,   ecure , rege,

et guberna.

Amen.

Prayer of Protection from the Babylonian

Talmud

O Lord, grant that this night we may be in

peace. And that in the morning may we also be

in peace. May our daytime be cloaked in your

peace.

Protect us and inspire us to think and act only

out of love.

Keep far from us all evil; may our paths be free

from all obstacles from when we go out until we

return home.

Prayer of Empowering

Father God as we stand here before you we acknowledge our utter lack of power in confronting the possible evil that stands before us.

But we trust not in ourselves but in Christ, the forgiveness of His Blood and the power of His Spirit.

Right now we hand this battle in which we are about to participate over to You. As your Word says, 'Not by might, not by power, but by My Spirit says the Lord'.

We ask Your presence to fill us, Your wisdom to guide us and Your Spirit's power to protect us. Amen.

Prayer of Protection

Father we come before you in the Name of the
Lord Jesus Christ of Nazareth, only begotten
Son of God. We ask for Your protection against
any evil influence as we enter this building.
Protect our hearts, protect our minds, protect our
bodies and protect those who strive with us in
the Name and in the Blood of the Lord Jesus
Christ.

Protect our ignorance from being used by the
enemy in order to afflict us and harass us. We
ask Your wisdom, love, and discernment guide
our steps as we help those who cannot help
themselves. In Jesus' Name, Amen.

Responsive Prayer of Protection

(Practitioner)   **(Associate)**

God be with us.   *As we trust in Thee.*

God empower us.   *As we surrender to Thee.*

God guide us.   *As we seek Your Face.*

God protect us.   *As we rest in Thee*

(In Unison)

For the weapons of our warfare are not carnal,

but mighty through God to the pulling down of

strong holds;

 Casting down imaginations, and every high

thing that exalteth itself against the knowledge

of God, and bringing into captivity every

thought to the obedience of Christ. Amen.

Responsive Prayer of Empowerment

Practitioner: Jesus said, *"And these signs shall follow them that believe; In my name shall they cast out devils."*

Associates: Thou believest that there is one God; thou doest well: the devils also believe, and tremble.

Practitioner: Now unto him that is able to do exceeding abundantly above all that we ask or think, according to the power that worketh in us, Unto him be glory in the church by Christ Jesus throughout all ages, world without end. Amen.

A Prayer of St. Columba

What need I fear?

Alone with none but Thee, my God,

I journey on my way;

What need I fear when Thou art near,

Oh King of night and day?

More safe am I within Thy hand

Than if a host did round me stand.

Amen

An Ancient Celtic Invocation

I will go in the name of God,

In likeness of deer, in likeness of horse,

In likeness of serpent, in likeness of king,

Stronger am I than all persons.

The hand of God keeping me,

The love of Christ in my veins,

The strong Spirit bathing me,

The Three shielding and aiding me,

The Three shielding and aiding me;

The hand of Spirit bathing me,

The Three each step aiding me.

The Lorica of Saint Patrick

The Lorica of Saint Patrick is an ancient invocation of the Holy Trinity, originally in Gaelic and attributed to Saint Patrick.

The word Lorica is a Latin term meaning shield or breastplate.

This is an ancient Irish prayer for protection against evil and its manifestation both physical and spiritual.

Presented in English and Gaelic, this ancient prayer can inspire faith and confidence as you step into the unknown:

English

I arise today

Through a mighty strength, the invocation of the

Trinity,

Through a belief in the Threeness,

Through confession of the Oneness

Of the Creator of creation.

I arise today

Through the strength of Christ with his baptism,

Through the strength of his crucifixion with his

burial,

Through the strength of his resurrection with his

ascension

Through the strength of his decent for the

Judgement of doom.

Gaelic

A tomriug   ecure

niurt tréun:

togairm Trindóit

faístin Oendatad,

i nDúlemon dáil.

Atomriug   ecure

niurt gene Críst cona bathius,

niurt a chrochtho cona adnacul,

niurt a essérgi cona fhresgabáil,

niurt a thoíniudo fri brithemnas mbrátho.

English

I arise today

Through the strength of the love of Cherubim

In obedience to the Angels,

In the service of the Archangels,

In hope of resurrection to meet with reward,

In prayers of patriarchs,

In predictions of prophets,

In preaching of Apostles,

In faiths of confessors,

In innocence of Holy Virgins,

In deeds of righteous men.

Gaelic

Atomriug   ecure

niurt gráid hiruphin,

i n-aurlataid aingel,

i frestul inna n-archaingel,

i freiscisin esséirgi

ar chiunn fochraicce,

i n-ernaigthib uasalathrach,

i tairchetlaib fáithe,

i preceptaib apstal,

i n-iresaib foísmedach,

i n-enccai noebingen,

i ngnímaib fer firén.

English

I arise today

Through the strength of heaven;

Light of the sun,

Splendor of fire,

Speed of lightning,

Swiftness of the wind,

Depth of the sea,

Stability of the earth,

Firmness of the rock.

Gaelic

Atomriug   ecure

niurt nime,

soilsi gréne,

étrochtai éscai,

áni thened,

déni lóchet,

luaithi gaíthe,

fudomnai mara,

tairismigi thalman,

cobsaidi ailech.

English

I arise today

Through God's strength to pilot me:

God's might to uphold me,

God's wisdom to guide me

God's eye to look before me,

God's ear to hear me,

God's word to speak for me,

God's hand to guard me,

God's way to lie before me,

God's host to secure me

against snares of devils against temptations of

vices against inclinations of nature

against everyone who shall wish me ill,

afar and anear,

alone and in a crowd.

Gaelic

Atomriug   ecure

niurt Dé dom luamairecht.

Cumachtae nDé dom chumgabáil,

ciall Dé dom inthús,

rose nDé dom remcisiu,

cluas Dé dom étsecht,

briathar Dé dom erlabrai,

lám Dé dom imdegail,

intech Dé dom remthechtas,

sciath Dé dom imdítin, sochraite Dé dom anacul

ar intledaib demnae, ar aslagib dualche,

ar forimthechtaib aicnid,

ar cech duine mídúthrastar dam,

i céin ocus i n-ocus,

i n'uathud ocus i sochaidi.

English

A summon today all these powers between me
and these evils

Against every cruel and merciless power that
may oppose my body and my soul,

Against incantations of false prophets,

Against black laws of heathenry,

Against false laws of heretics,

Against craft of idolatry,

Against spells of women and smiths and
wizards,

Against every knowledge that endangers man's
body and soul.

Gaelic

Tocuiriur etrum   ecure inna uili nert-so

fri cech nert n-amnas n-étrocar frista-i dom

churp ocus dom anmain,

fri tinchetla sa-ibfh-aithe,

fri dubrechtu gentliuchtae,

fri saíbrechtu heretecdae,

fri imchellacht n-ídlachtae,

fri brichtu ban ocus goban ocus druad,

fri cech fiss arachuille corp ocus anmain duini.

English

Christ to protect me today

against poison, against burning,

against drowning, against wounding,

so that there may come abundance of reward.

Christ with me, Christ before me, Christ behind

me, Christ in me, Christ beneath me, Christ

above me, Christ on my right, Christ on my left

Christ where I lie, Christ where I sit, Christ

where I arise

Christ in the heart of every man who thinks of

me,

Christ in the mouth of every man who speaks of

me,

Christ in every eye that sees me,

Christ in every ear that hears me.

Gaelic

Crist dom imdegail ecure

ar neim, ar loscud, ar bádud, ar guin,

condom-thair ilar fochraicce.

Críst limm, Críst reum, Críst im degaid,

Críst indium, Críst ísum, Críst uasum,

Críst desum, Críst tuathum,

Críst i llius, Críst i sius, Críst i n-erus,

Críst i cridiu cech duini immumrorda,

Críst ecure cech oín rodom-labrathar,

Críst i cech rusc nonom-dercathar,

Críst i cech cluais rodom-chloathar.

English

I arise today

Through a mighty strength, the invocation of the

Trinity,

Through belief in the Thrones,

Through confession of the Oneness

Towards the Creator.

Salvation is of the Lord

Salvation is of the Lord

Salvation is of Christ

May thy salvation, O Lord, be ever with us.

Gaelic

Atomriug   ecure

niurt tréun:

togairm Trindóit,

cretim Treodatad,

faístin Oendatad,

i nDúlemon dáil.

Domini est salus,

Domini est salus,

Christi est salusñ

salus tua, Domine, sit   ecure nobiscum.

Sealing Prayers

General Sealing Prayer 1 (*Censer use*)

We seal off this house in the Name of the Lord

Jesus Christ, only begotten Son of God.

What is here cannot leave.

None may enter.

We call upon the host of heaven to guard these

walls and prevent all coming and going.

We seal the North I

We seal the South I

We seal the East I

We seal the West I

Above and below

Lord of Hosts cut off this room from

Principalities and Powers. Amen

General Sealing Prayer 2

In the name of Jesus Christ, I bind

all spirits of the air, water, ground, underground

and Hades.

I bind any and all emissaries of Satan and claim

the Blood of Jesus on the air, the water, the

ground and all living things, on the ethereal and

unseen.

In the name of The Lord Jesus Christ, I forbid

any spirit from communication with any other

or helping any other or receiving help from any

other in any way.

We bind this place through the Blood of Jesus

Christ, Lord of Hosts. Amen.

Power of the Name Prayer with Holy Water

In the Name of the Lord Jesus Christ we pray:

We seal this door by the power of your name

(anoint water on every door as all say in unison)

In the Name of the Father, Son and Holy Spirit.

We seal this window by the power of your name

(anoint water on every window and repeat)

In the Name of the Father, Son and Holy Spirit.

We seal all of the North (anoint), East (anoint),

South (anoint), West (anoint), above and below

In the Name of the Father, Son and Holy Spirit

(anoint floor)

By the Power of the risen Lord Jesus Christ,

through the power of His Spirit to the glory of

the Father. Amen

Sealing off the power of the Occult

God is our strength

God is our refuge

God is our fortress

Through the power of Christ

All evil here in under His authority

The minions of evil have no power

Be it through witchcraft, divination, sorcery or

fellowship with familiars.

Jesus Christ, who is over all principalities and

powers is Lord over this building.

By His power this place is sealed and all evil

that resides must stay, and that which does not

abide here cannot enter. Amen

African Prayer of Sealing (English)

Jesus Blood has been given

The Prince of Peace has come to the world

The King is coming.

A sacrifice has been given.

God loves us.

There is power in the Blood of Jesus

He shall come to judge the quick and the dead.

This is sealed by the Blood.

This is His.

Evil has no power.

African Prayer of Sealing (African Jula)

Yesu joli bonna

Hereba nana dien bee ka hereba nana

Masaya be na

Saraka dira, dien bee ka saraka dira

Ala b'an kanu

Fangaba be Yesu joli la

Ka nyanamanw ni suw bee kiiritige

A joli ye ne saniya

Ala y'an

Nii senu yere jurumu ban.

Choral sealing prayer

By the Lord a wall has been formed

Not of brick or mortar, but of Spirit and power

By the Lord a barricade is raised

That no evil shall pass

By the Lord evil is made powerless

Like a beast caught in a trap

By the Lord the righteous are empowered

To drive out all unclean spirits

By the Lord they shall have no help

As they are driven into the pit

And by the Lord we shall have victory

Amen

Lord of Powers Prayer

Lord of the Powers be with us,

 in times of distress You are our help.

Lord of the Powers, have mercy on us,

we look unto You for protection.

Lord of Powers we trust in You,

gather Your hosts around us

prevent the coming and going of all spirits.

Lord of Powers we praise You,

In the name of your only begotten Son

Jesus Christ, Amen.

Lord of Hosts Prayer (English)

Lord of Hosts grant us your angels

To guard these doorways

Lord of Hosts grant us your Seraphim

To hold back evil with flaming swords

Lord of Hosts grant us your power

And render the evil one powerless

Lord of Hosts may your Spirit be with us

And give us strength

Amen

Lord of Hosts Prayer (Latin)

Dominus exercituum tribuo nos   ecure angelus

Custodio illa ianua

Dominus exercituum tribuo nos   ecure

Seraphim Retineo malum per flamma mucro

Dominus exercituum tribuo nos   ecure vox

Quod   ecu malum unus inops

Dominus exercituum   ecure Phasmatis exsisto

nobis Quod tribuo nos vires

Amen

Biblical Passages

Group A Scriptures for preparation, to instill faith.

1 John 3:3-4 (English)

"And every spirit that confesseth not that Jesus Christ is come in the flesh is not of God: and this is that spirit of antichrist, whereof ye have heard that it should come; and even now already is it in the world.

Ye are of God, little children, and have overcome them: because greater is he that is in you, than he that is in the world."

1 John 3:3-4 (Latin)

Et omnis spíritus qui solvit Jesum, ex Deo non est, et hic est antichrístus, de quo audístis quóniam venit, et nunc jam in mundo est.

Vos ex Deo estis filíoli, et vicístis eum, quóniam major est qui in vobis est, quam qui in mundo.

Ephesians 6:10-18 (English)

"Be strong in the Lord and in his mighty power. Put on the full armor of God so that you can take your stand against the devil's schemes. For our struggle is not against flesh and blood, but against the rulers, against the authorities, against the powers of this dark world and against the spiritual forces of evil in the heavenly realms.

Therefore put on the full armor of God, so that when the day of evil comes, you may be able to stand your ground, and after you have done everything, to stand. Stand firm then, with the belt of truth buckled around your waist, with the breastplate of righteousness in place, and with your feet fitted with the readiness that comes from the gospel of peace.

In addition to all this, take up the shield of faith, with which you can extinguish all the flaming arrows of the evil one. Take the helmet of salvation and the sword of the Spirit, which is the word of God. And pray in the Spirit on all occasions with all kinds of prayers and requests."

Ephesians 6:10-18 (Latin)

Confortámini in Dómino, et in ecure ou virtútis ejus. Indúite vos armatúram Dei, ut possítis stare advérsus insídias diáboli : quóniam non est nobis colluctátio advérsus carnem et sánguinem, sed advérsus príncipes, et potestátes, advérsus mundi rectóres tenebrárum harum, contra spirituália nequítiæ, in cæléstibus.

 Proptérea ecure ou armatúram Dei, ut possítis resístere in die malo, et in ecure perfécti stare. State ergo succíncti lumbos vestros in veritáte, et indúti lorícam justítiæ, et calceáti pedes in præparatióne Evangélii pacis,

In ecure   suméntes scutum fídei, in quo possítis ómnia tela nequíssimi ígnea extínguere : et gáleam salútis assúmite, et gládium spíritus (quod est verbum Dei), per omnem oratiónem et obsecratiónem orántes omni témpore in spíritu :

Romans 8:38-39 (English)

"For I am persuaded, that neither death, nor life, nor angels, nor principalities, nor powers, nor things present, nor things to come,

Nor height, nor depth, nor any other creature, shall be able to separate us from the love of God, which is in Christ Jesus our Lord."

Romans 8:38-39 (Latin)

Certus sum enim quia neque mors, neque vita, neque ángeli, neque principátus, neque virtútes, neque instántia, neque   ecure, neque   ecure   ou,

neque   ecure   o, neque profúndum, neque creatúra ália póterit nos separáre a caritáte Dei, quæ est in Christo Jesu Dómino nostro.

Psalm 27:1-5 (English)

The LORD is my light and my salvation; whom shall I fear? The LORD is the strength of my life; of whom shall I be afraid?

When the wicked, even mine enemies and my foes, came upon me to eat up my flesh, they stumbled and fell.

Though a host should encamp against me, my heart shall not fear: though war should rise against me, in this will I be confident.

One thing have I desired of the LORD, that will I seek after; that I may dwell in the house of the LORD all the days of my life, to behold the beauty of the LORD, and to enquire in his temple.

For in the time of trouble he shall hide me in his pavilion: in the secret of his tabernacle shall he hide me; he shall set me up upon a rock.

Psalm 27:1-5 (Latin)

Dóminus illuminátio mea et salus mea :
quem timébo ?
Dóminus   ecure   ou vitæ meæ :
a quo trepidábo ?

Dum aprópiant super me nocéntes ut
edant carnes meas,
qui tríbulant me inimíci mei,
ipsi infirmáti sunt et cecidérunt.

Si consístant advérsum me castra, non
timébit cor meum ;
si exsúrgat advérsum me prǽlium, in
hoc ego sperábo.

Unam pétii a Dómino, hanc requíram,
ut inhábitem in domo Dómini   ecure
diébus vitæ meæ ;
ut vídeam voluptátem Dómini, et
vísitem templum ejus.

Quóniam abscóndit me in tabernáculo
suo ;
in die malórum protéxit me in
abscóndito tabernáculi sui.

Psalm 44:4-8, 25-26 (English)

Thou art my King, O God: command
deliverances for Jacob.

Through thee will we push down our enemies:
through thy name will we tread them under that
rise up against us.

For I will not trust in my bow, neither shall my
sword save me.

But thou hast saved us from our enemies, and
hast put them to shame that hated us.

In God we boast all the day long, and praise thy
name for ever. Selah.

For our soul is bowed down to the dust: our
belly cleaveth unto the earth.

Arise for our help, and redeem us for thy
mercies' sake.

Psalm 44:4-8, 25-26 (Latin)

ecur ipse rex meus et Deus meus,
qui mandas ecure Jacob.

In te inimícos nostros ventilábimus
cornu,
et in   ecure   tuo spernémus ecure   ous
in nobis.

Non enim in arcu meo sperábo,
et gládius meus non salvábit me :

salvásti enim nos de affligéntibus nos,
et odiéntes nos confudísti.

In Deo laudábimur tota die, et in ecure
tuo confitébimur in sǽculum.

Quóniam   ecure   ou est in púlvere
   ecur nostra ;
conglutinátus est in terra venter noster.

Exsúrge, Dómine, ádjuva nos,
t rédime nos propter nomen tuum.

Psalm 46:1-3, 7, 10-11 (English)

God is our refuge and strength, a very present
help in trouble.

Therefore will not we fear, though the earth be
removed, and though the mountains be carried
into the midst of the sea;

Though the waters thereof roar and be troubled,
though the mountains shake with the swelling
thereof. Selah.

The LORD of hosts is with us;
the God of Jacob is our refuge. Selah.

Be still, and know that I am God: I will be
exalted among the heathen, I will be exalted in
the earth.

The LORD of hosts is with us; the God of
Jacob is our refuge. Selah.

Psalm 46:1-3, 7, 10-11 (Latin)

Deus noster refúgium et virtus ;
adjútor in tribulatiónibus quæ
invenérunt nos nimis.

Proptérea non timébimus dum turbábitur
terra,
et transferéntur montes in cor maris.

Sonuérunt, et turbátæ sunt aquæ eórum ;
conturbáti sunt montes in fortitúdine
ejus.

Dóminus virtútum nobíscum ;
 suscéptor noster Deus Jacob.

Vacáte, et vidéte quóniam ego sum
Deus ;
exaltábor in géntibus, et exaltábor in
terra.

Dóminus virtútum nobíscum ;
suscéptor noster Deus Jacob.

Psalm 64 (English)

Hear my voice, O God, in my prayer: preserve
my life from fear of the enemy.

Hide me from the secret counsel of the wicked;
from the insurrection of the workers of iniquity:

They search out iniquities; they accomplish a
diligent search: both the inward thought of
every one of them, and the heart, is deep.

But God shall shoot at them with an arrow;
suddenly shall they be wounded.

So they shall make their own tongue to fall upon
themselves: all that see them shall flee away.

And all men shall fear, and shall declare the
work of God; for they shall wisely consider of
his doing.

The righteous shall be glad in the LORD, and
shall trust in him; and all the upright in heart
shall glory.

Psalm 64 (Latin)

Exáudi, Deus, oratiónem meam cum
déprecor ;
a timóre inimíci éripe ánimam meam.

Protexísti me a convéntu malignántium,
a multitúdine operántium iniquitátem.

Scrutáti sunt iniquitátes ;
defecérunt scrutántes scrutínio.
Accédet homo ad cor altum,

et exaltábitur Deus.
Sagíttæ parvulórum factæ sunt plagæ
eórum,

et infirmátæ sunt contra eos linguæ
eórum. Conturbáti sunt omnes qui
vidébant eos,

et tímuit omnis homo.
Et annuntiavérunt   ecur Dei,
et facta ejus intellexérunt.

Lætábitur   ecure in Dómino, et sperábit
in eo, et laudabúntur omnes recti corde.

Psalm 67 (English)

God be merciful unto us, and bless us; and cause his face to shine upon us; Selah.

That thy way may be known upon earth, thy saving health among all nations.

Let the people praise thee, O God; let all the people praise thee.

O let the nations be glad and sing for joy: for thou shalt judge the people righteously, and govern the nations upon earth. Selah.

Let the people praise thee, O God; let all the people praise thee.

Then shall the earth yield her increase; and God, even our own God, shall bless us.

God shall bless us; and all the ends of the earth shall fear him.

Psalm 67 (Latin)

Deus misereátur   ecure   , et benedícat
nobis ;
illúminet vultum suum super nos, et
misereátur   ecure   :

ut cognoscámus in terra viam tuam,
in   ecure   géntibus salutáre tuum.

Confiteántur tibi pópuli, Deus :
confiteántur tibi pópuli omnes.

Lætêntur et exsúltent gentes,
quóniam júdicas pópulos in æquitáte,
et gentes in terra dírigis.

Confiteántur tibi pópuli, Deus :
confiteántur tibi pópuli omnes.

Terra dedit fructum suum :
benedícat nos Deus, Deus noster !

Benedícat nos Deus,
et métuant eum omnes fines terræ.

Psalm 98 (English)

O sing unto the LORD a new song; for he hath done marvelous things: his right hand, and his holy arm, hath gotten him the victory.

The LORD hath made known his salvation: all the ends of the earth have seen the salvation of our God.

Make a joyful noise unto the LORD, all the earth: make a loud noise, and rejoice, and sing praise.

Sing unto the LORD with the harp; with the harp, and the voice of a psalm.

With trumpets and sound of cornet make a joyful noise before the LORD, the King.

Let the sea roar, and the fullness thereof; the world, and they that dwell therein.

Let the floods clap their hands: let the hills be joyful together

Before the LORD; for he cometh to judge the earth: with righteousness shall he judge the world, and the people with equity.

Psalm 98 (Latin)

Cantáte Dómino cánticum novum,
quia mirabília fecit.
Salvávit sibi déxtera ejus,
et   ecure   o sanctum ejus.

Notum fecit Dóminus salutáre suum ;
Vidérunt omnes   ecure   terræ
salutáre Dei   ecure   .

Jubiláte Deo, omnis terra ;
   ecure   , et exsultáte, et psállite.

Psállite Dómino in   ecure   ;
in   ecure   et voce psalmi ;

in tubis ductílibus, et voce tubæ córneæ.
Jubiláte in   ecure   ous   ecur Dómini :

moveátur mare, et   ecure   ou ejus ;
orbis   ecure   ou, et qui   ecure   o in
eo.

Flúmina plaudent manu ; simul montes
exsultábunt

a   ecure   ous Dómini :
quóniam venit judicáre terram.
Judicábit orbem   ecure   ou in justítia,
et pópulos in æquitáte.

Isaiah 40:10-11, 29-31 (English)

Behold, the Lord GOD will come with strong hand, and his arm shall rule for him: behold, his reward is with him, and his work before him.

He shall feed his flock like a shepherd: he shall gather the lambs with his arm, and carry them in his bosom, and shall gently lead those that are with young.

He giveth power to the faint; and to them that have no might he increaseth strength.

Even the youths shall faint and be weary, and the young men shall utterly fall:

But they that wait upon the LORD shall renew their strength; they shall mount up with wings as eagles; they shall run, and not be weary; and they shall walk, and not faint.

Isaiah 40:10-11, 29-31 (Latin)

ecce Dóminus Deus in fortitúdine
véniet,
et ecure o ejus dominábitur :
ecce merces ejus cum eo,
et opus illíus coram illo.

Sicut pastor gregem suum pascet,
in bráchio suo congregábit agnos,
et in sinu suo levábit ; fœtas ipse
portábit.

Qui dat lasso virtútem,
et his qui non sunt, fortitúdinem et robur
multíplicat.

Defícient púeri, et laborábunt,
et júvenes in infirmitáte cadent ;

qui autem ecure in Dómino
mutábunt fortitúdinem,
assúment pennas sicut áquilæ :
current et non laborábunt,
ambulábunt et non ecure ou.

Jeremiah 20: 11-13 (English)

But the LORD is with me as a mighty terrible
one: therefore my persecutors shall stumble,

and they shall not prevail: they shall be greatly
ashamed; for they shall not prosper:

their everlasting confusion shall never be
forgotten.

But, O LORD of hosts, that triest the righteous,
and seest the reins and the heart,

let me see thy vengeance on them: for unto thee
have I opened my cause.

Sing unto the LORD, praise ye the LORD:

for he hath delivered the soul of the poor from
the hand of evildoers.

Jeremiah 20:11-13 (Latin)

Dóminus autem mecum est, quasi
bellátor fortis :

idcírco qui persequúntur me cadent,
et infírmi erunt :

confundéntur veheménter,
quia non intellexérunt ecure ous
sempitérnum,
quod numquam delébitur.

Et tu, Dómine exercítuum, probátor
justi,
qui vides renes et cor,

vídeam, quæso, ultiónem tuam ex eis :
tibi enim revelávi causam meam.

Cantáte Dómino,
laudáte Dóminum,

quia liberávit ánimam páuperis de manu
malórum.

Matthew 10:16, 27-31 (English)

Behold, I send you forth as sheep in the midst of wolves: be ye therefore wise as serpents, and harmless as doves.

What I tell you in darkness, that speak ye in light: and what ye hear in the ear, that preach ye upon the housetops.

And fear not them which kill the body, but are not able to kill the soul: but rather fear him which is able to destroy both soul and body in hell.

Are not two sparrows sold for a farthing? And one of them shall not fall on the ground without your Father.

But the very hairs of your head are all numbered.

Matthew 10:16, 27-31 (Latin)

Ecce ego mitto vos sicut oves in médio
lupórum. Estóte ergo prudéntes sicut   ecure o,
et símplices sicut colúmbæ

Quod dico vobis in ténebris, dícite in
lúmine : et quod in aure audítis, prædicáte
super tecta.

Et nolíte timére eos qui   ecure o corpus,
ánimam autem non possunt occídere : sed
pótius timéte eum, qui potest et ánimam et
corpus pérdere in gehénnam.

Nonne duo   ecure   asse véneunt ? et unus
ex illis non cadet super terram sine Patre
vestro.

Vestri autem capílli cápitis omnes
    ecure o sunt.

Nolíte ergo timére : multis passéribus
melióres estis vos.

John 3:16-21 (English)

For God so loved the world, that he gave his only begotten Son, that whosoever believeth in him should not perish, but have everlasting life.

For God sent not his Son into the world to condemn the world; but that the world through him might be saved.

He that believeth on him is not condemned: but he that believeth not is condemned already, because he hath not believed in the name of the only begotten Son of God.

And this is the condemnation, that light is come into the world, and men loved darkness rather than light, because their deeds were evil.

For every one that doeth evil hates the light, neither cometh to the light, lest his deeds should be reproved.

But he that doeth truth cometh to the light, that his deeds may be made manifest, that they are wrought in God.

John 3:16-21 (Latin)

Sic enim Deus diléxit mundum, ut Fílium suum
unigénitum daret : ut omnis qui credit in eum,
non péreat, sed hábeat vitam ætérnam.

Non enim misit Deus Fílium suum in mundum,
ut júdicet mundum, sed ut salvétur mundus per
ipsum.

Qui credit in eum, non judicátur ; qui autem non
credit, jam judicátus est : quia non credit in
    ecure   unigéniti Fílii Dei.

Hoc est autem judícium : quia lux venit in
mundum, et dilexérunt   ecure   o magis
ténebras quam lucem :   ecure enim eórum mala
    ecur.

Omnis enim qui male agit, odit lucem, et non
venit ad lucem, ut non arguántur   ecur ejus :

qui autem facit veritátem, venit ad lucem, ut
manifesténtur   ecur ejus, quia in Deo sunt
facta.

John 15: 1, 3-4,7-11 (English)

I am the true vine, and my Father is the
husbandman.

Now ye are clean through the word which I
have spoken unto you.

Abide in me, and I in you. As the branch cannot
bear fruit of itself, except it abide in the vine; no
more can ye, except ye abide in me.

If ye abide in me, and my words abide in you,
ye shall ask what ye will, and it shall be done
unto you.

Herein is my Father glorified, that ye bear much
fruit; so shall ye be my disciples.

As the Father hath loved me, so have I loved
you: continue ye in my love.

If ye keep my commandments, ye shall abide in
my love; even as I have kept my Father's
commandments, and abide in his love.

These things have I spoken unto you, that my
joy might remain in you, and that your joy
might be full.

John 15:1, 3-4, 7-11 (Latin)

Ego sum vitis vera, et Pater meus agrícola est

Jam vos mundi estis propter sermónem quem locútus sum vobis.

Manéte in me, et ego in vobis. Sicut palmes non potest ferre fructum a semetípso, nisi mánserit in vite, sic nec vos, nisi in me manséritis

Si manséritis in me, et verba mea in vobis mánserint, quodcúmque voluéritis petétis, et fiet vobis.

In hoc clarificátus est Pater meus, ut fructum plúrimum afferátis, et efficiámini mei discípuli.

Sicut diléxit me Pater, et ego diléxi vos. Manéte in dilectióne mea.

Si præcépta mea servavéritis, manébitis in dilectióne mea, sicut et ego Patris mei præcépta servávi, et máneo in ejus dilectióne.

Hæc locútus sum vobis : ut gáudium meum in vobis sit, et gáudium vestrum impleátur

Romans 5: 1-5 (English)

Therefore being justified by faith, we have
peace with God through our Lord Jesus Christ:

By whom also we have access by faith into this
grace wherein we stand, and rejoice in hope of
the glory of God.

And not only so, but we glory in tribulations
also: knowing that tribulation worketh patience;

And patience, experience; and experience, hope:

And hope maketh not ashamed; because the
love of God is shed abroad in our hearts by the
Holy Ghost which is given unto us.

Romans 5:1-5 (Latin)

Justificáti ergo ex fide, pacem habeámus ad
Deum per Dóminum nostrum Jesum Christum :

per quem et habémus accéssum per fidem in
grátiam istam, in qua stamus, et gloriámur in spe
glóriæ filiórum Dei.

Non solum autem, sed et gloriámur in
tribulatiónibus : sciéntes quod   ecure   ous
patiéntiam   ecure   o :

patiéntia autem probatiónem,   ecure   ou vero
spem,

spes autem non confúndit : quia   ecure   Dei
diffúsa est in córdibus nostris per Spíritum
Sanctum, qui datus est nobis

Romans 8:1-4, 15 (English)

There is therefore now no condemnation to them which are in Christ Jesus, who walk not after the flesh, but after the Spirit.

For the law of the Spirit of life in Christ Jesus hath made me free from the law of sin and death.

For what the law could not do, in that it was weak through the flesh, God sending his own Son in the likeness of sinful flesh, and for sin, condemned sin in the flesh:

That the righteousness of the law might be fulfilled in us, who walk not after the flesh, but after the Spirit

For ye have not received the spirit of bondage again to fear; but ye have received the Spirit of adoption, whereby we cry, Abba, Father.

Romans 8:1-4, 15 (Latin)

Nihil ergo nunc damnatiónis est iis qui sunt in
Christo Jesu : qui non secúndum carnem
   ecure o.

Lex enim spíritus vitæ in Christo Jesu liberávit
me a lege peccáti et mortis.

Nam quod impossíbile erat legi, in quo
infirmabátur per carnem : Deus Fílium suum
mittens in similitúdinem carnis peccáti et de
peccáto, damnávit peccátum in carne,

ut   ecure ous   n legis implerétur in nobis,
qui non secúndum carnem ambulámus, sed
secúndum spíritum

Non enim accepístis spíritum servitútis íterum in
timóre, sed accepístis spíritum adoptiónis
filiórum, in quo clamámus : Abba (Páter).

2 Corinthians 10:3-6 (English)

For though we walk in the flesh, we do not war after the flesh:

(For the weapons of our warfare are not carnal, but mighty through God to the pulling down of strong holds;)

Casting down imaginations, and every high thing that exalteth itself against the knowledge of God, and bringing into captivity every thought to the obedience of Christ;

And having in a readiness to revenge all disobedience, when your obedience is fulfilled.

2 Corintians 10:3-6 (Latin)

In carne enim ambulántes, non secúndum
carnem militámus.

Nam arma milítiæ nostræ non carnália sunt, sed
ecure ou Deo ad destructiónem munitiónum,
consília destruéntes,

et omnem altitúdinem extolléntem se advérsus
sciéntiam Dei, et in captivitátem redigéntes
omnem intelléctum in obséquium Christi,

et in promptu habéntes ulcísci omnem
inobediéntiam, cum impléta fúerit vestra
obediéntia.

1 Peter 5:6-11 (English)

Humble yourselves therefore under the mighty hand of God, that he may exalt you in due time:

Casting all your care upon him; for he careth for you.

Be sober, be vigilant; because your adversary the devil, as a roaring lion, walketh about, seeking whom he may devour:

Whom resist stedfast in the faith, knowing that the same afflictions are accomplished in your brethren that are in the world.

But the God of all grace, who hath called us unto his eternal glory by Christ Jesus, after that ye have suffered a while, make you perfect, stablish, strengthen, settle you.

To him be glory and dominion for ever and ever. Amen.

1 Peter 5:6-11 (Latin)

Humiliámini ígitur sub poténti manu Dei, ut vos
exáltet in témpore visitatiónis :

omnem sollicitúdinem vestram projiciéntes in
eum, quóniam ipsi cura est de vobis.

Sóbrii estóte, et vigiláte : quia   ecure   ous
vester diábolus tamquam leo rúgiens   ecure   ,
quærens quem dévoret :

cui resístite fortes in fide : sciéntes eámdem
passiónem ei quæ in mundo est vestræ
fraternitáti fíeri.

Deus autem omnis grátiæ, qui vocávit nos in
ætérnam suam glóriam in Christo Jesu,
   ecure   passos ipse perfíciet, confirmábit,
solidabítque.

Ipsi glória, et impérium in sǽcula sæculórum.
Amen.

1 John 4:1-4 (English)

Beloved, believe not every spirit, but try the spirits whether they are of God: because many false prophets are gone out into the world.

Hereby know ye the Spirit of God: Every spirit that confesseth that Jesus Christ is come in the flesh is of God:

And every spirit that confesseth not that Jesus Christ is come in the flesh is not of God: and this is that spirit of antichrist, whereof ye have heard that it should come; and even now already is it in the world.

Ye are of God, little children, and have overcome them: because greater is he that is in you, than he that is in the world.

1 John 4:1-4 (Latin)

Caríssimi, nolíte omni spirítui crédere, sed
  ecure spíritus si ex Deo sint : quóniam multi
pseudoprophétæ exiérunt in mundum.

In hoc cognoscítur Spíritus Dei : omnis spíritus
qui confitétur Jesum Christum in carne venísse,
ex Deo est :

et omnis spíritus qui solvit Jesum, ex Deo non
est, et hic est antichrístus, de quo audístis
quóniam venit, et nunc jam in mundo est.

 Vos ex Deo estis filíoli, et vicístis eum,
quóniam major est qui in vobis est, quam qui in
mundo

James 4:7-10 (English)

Submit yourselves therefore to God. Resist the devil, and he will flee from you.

Draw nigh to God, and he will draw nigh to you. Cleanse your hands, ye sinners; and purify your hearts, ye double minded.

Be afflicted, and mourn, and weep: let your laughter be turned to mourning, and your joy to heaviness.

Humble yourselves in the sight of the Lord, and he shall lift you up.

James 4:7-10 (Latin)

Súbditi ergo estóte Deo, resístite autem diábolo, et fúgiet a vobis.

 Appropinquáte Deo, et appropinquábit vobis. Emundáte manus, peccatóres : et purificáte corda, dúplices ánimo.

Míseri estóte, et lugéte, et ploráte : risus vester in luctum convertátur, et gáudium in mœrórem.

Humiliámini in   ecure   ous Dómini, et exaltábit vos.

Group B Scriptures to rebuke the entity and
establish dominance.

James 2:19 (English)

Thou believest that there is one God; thou doest
well: the devils also believe, and tremble.

James 2:19 (Latin)

Tu credis quóniam unus est Deus : bene facis :
et dǽmones credunt, et contremíscunt.

Revelation 20:10 (English)

And the devil that deceived them was cast into
the lake of fire and brimstone, where the beast
and the false prophet are, and shall be tormented
day and night for ever and ever.

Revelation 20:10 (Latin)

et diábolus, qui seducébat eos, missus est in
stagnum ignis, et sulphúris, ubi et béstia et
pseudoprophéta cruciabúntur die ac nocte in
sǽcula sæculórum.

Colossians 2:13-15 (English)

And you, being dead in your sins and the uncircumcision of your flesh, hath he quickened together with him, having forgiven you all trespasses;

Blotting out the handwriting of ordinances that was against us, which was contrary to us, and took it out of the way, nailing it to his cross;

And having spoiled principalities and powers, he made a shew of them openly, triumphing over them in it.

Colossians 2:13-15 (Latin)

Et vos cum mórtui essétis in delíctis, et præpútio carnis vestræ, convivificávit cum illo, ecure vobis ómnia delícta :

delens quod advérsus ecure o chirográphum decréti, quod erat contrárium nobis, et ipsum tulit de médio, áffigens illud cruci :

et expólians principátus, et potestátes tradúxit confidénter, palam triúmphans illos in semetípso.

Hebrews 4:12-13 (English)

For the word of God is quick, and powerful, and
sharper than any two edged sword, piercing
even to the dividing asunder of soul and spirit,
and of the joints and marrow, and is a discerner
of the thoughts and intents of the heart.

 Neither is there any creature that is not manifest
in his sight: but all things are naked and opened
unto the eyes of him with whom we have to do.

Hebrews 4:12-13 (Latin)

Vivus est enim sermo Dei, et éfficax et
penetrabílior omni gládio ancípiti : et pertíngens
usque ad divisiónem ánimæ ac spíritus :
cómpagum quoque ac medullárum, et discrétor
cogitatiónum et intentiónum cordis.

 Et non est ulla creatúra invisíbilis in
    ecure   ous ejus : ómnia autem nuda et apérta
sunt óculis ejus, ad quem nobis sermo.

Revelation 20:11-15 (English)

And I saw a great white throne, and him that sat on it, from whose face the earth and the heaven fled away; and there was found no place for them.

And I saw the dead, small and great, stand before God; and the books were opened: and another book was opened, which is the book of life: and the dead were judged out of those things which were written in the books, according to their works.

And the sea gave up the dead which were in it; and death and hell delivered up the dead which were in them: and they were judged every man according to their works.

And death and hell were cast into the lake of fire. This is the second death.

And whosoever was not found written in the book of life was cast into the lake of fire.

Revelation 20:11-15 (Latin)

Et vidi thronum magnum cándidum, et
sedéntem super eum, a cujus   ecure   ous fugit
terra, et cælum, et locus non est invéntus eis.

Et vidi mórtuos, magnos et pusíllos, stantes in
   ecure   ous throni, et libri apérti sunt : et álius
liber apértus est, qui est vitæ : et judicáti sunt
mórtui ex his, quæ scripta   ecure in libris,
secúndum   ecur ipsórum :

et dedit mare mórtuos, qui in eo   ecure : et
mors et   ecure   o dedérunt mórtuos suos, qui
in ipsis   ecure : et judicátum est de síngulis
secúndum   ecur ipsórum.

Et   ecure   o et mors missi sunt in stagnum
ignis. Hæc est mors secúnda.

Et qui non invéntus est in libro vitæ scriptus,
missus est in stagnum ignis.

Psalm 52:2-7 (English)

The tongue deviseth mischiefs; like a sharp razor, working deceitfully.

Thou lovest evil more than good; and lying rather than to speak righteousness. Selah.

Thou lovest all devouring words, O thou deceitful tongue.

God shall likewise destroy thee for ever, he shall take thee away, and pluck thee out of thy dwelling place, and root thee out of the land of the living. Selah.

The righteous also shall see, and fear, and shall laugh at him:

Lo, this is the man that made not God his strength; but trusted in the abundance of his riches, and strengthened himself in his wickedness

Psalm 52:2-7 (Latin)

Tota die injustítiam cogitávit lingua tua ;
sicut novácula acúta fecísti dolum.

Dilexísti malítiam super benignitátem ;
iniquitátem magis quam loqui
æquitátem.

Dilexísti ómnia verba præcipitatiónis ;
lingua dolósa.

Proptérea Deus déstruet te in finem ;
evéllet te, et emigrábit te de tabernáculo
tuo,
et radícem tuam de terra vivéntium.

Vidébunt justi, et timébunt ;
et super eum ridébunt, et dicent :

Ecce homo qui non pósuit Deum
adjutórem suum ;
sed sperávit in multitúdine divitiárum
suárum, et præváluit in vanitáte sua.

Proverbs 10: 2-3; 25; 29-32 (English)

Treasures of wickedness profit nothing: but righteousness delivereth from death.

The LORD will not suffer the soul of the righteous to famish: but he casteth away the substance of the wicked.

As the whirlwind passeth, so is the wicked no more: but the righteous is an everlasting foundation.

The way of the LORD is strength to the upright: but destruction shall be to the workers of iniquity.

The righteous shall never be removed: but the wicked shall not inhabit the earth.

The mouth of the just bringeth forth wisdom: but the   ecure   tongue shall be cut out.

The lips of the righteous know what is acceptable: but the mouth of the wicked speaketh   ecure   ous   .

Proverbs 10: 2-3; 25; 29-32 (Latin)

Nil próderunt   ecure o impietátis,
justítia vero liberábit a morte.

Non afflíget Dóminus fame ánimam
justi, et insídias impiórum   ecure ou.

Quasi tempéstas tránsiens non erit
ímpius ;   ecure autem quasi
fundaméntum sempitérnum.

Fortitúdo símplicis via Dómini,
et pavor his qui operántur malum.

Justus in ætérnum non commovébitur,
ímpii autem non habitábunt super
terram.

Os justi   ecure ous sapiéntiam ;
lingua pravórum períbit.

Lábia justi consíderant plácita,
et os impiórum pervérsa.

Proverbs 15:7-11a; 29 (English)

The lips of the wise disperse knowledge: but the heart of the foolish doeth not so.

The sacrifice of the wicked is an abomination to the LORD: but the prayer of the upright is his delight.

The way of the wicked is an abomination unto the LORD: but he loveth him that followeth after righteousness.

Correction is grievous unto him that forsaketh the way: and he that hateth reproof shall die.

Hell and destruction are before the LORD

The LORD is far from the wicked: but he heareth the prayer of the righteous.

Proverbs 15:7-11a; 29 (Latin)

Lábia sapiéntium disseminábunt
sciéntiam ;
cor stultórum dissímile erit.

Víctimæ impiórum abominábiles
Dómino ;
vota justórum placabília.

Abominátio est Dómino via ímpii ;
qui séquitur justítiam dilígitur ab eo.

Doctrína mala deserénti viam vitæ ;
qui increpatiónes odit, moriétur.

Inférnus et   ecure   ou coram Dómino

Longe est Dóminus ab ímpiis,
  et   ecure   o justórum exáudiet.

Isaiah 14:9-15 (English)

Hell from beneath is moved for thee to meet thee at thy coming: it stirreth up the dead for thee, even all the chief ones of the earth; it hath raised up from their thrones all the kings of the nations.

All they shall speak and say unto thee, Art thou also become weak as we? Art thou become like unto us?

Thy pomp is brought down to the grave, and the noise of thy viols: the worm is spread under thee, and the worms cover thee.

How art thou fallen from heaven, O Lucifer, son of the morning! How art thou cut down to the ground, which didst weaken the nations!

For thou hast said in thine heart, I will ascend into heaven, I will exalt my throne above the stars of God: I will sit also upon the mount of the congregation, in the sides of the north:

I will ascend above the heights of the clouds; I will be like the most High.

Yet thou shalt be brought down to hell, to the sides of the pit.

121

Isaiah 14:9-15 (Latin)

Inférnus subter conturbátus est in
occúrsum advéntus tui ;suscitávit tibi
gigántes.Omnes príncipes terræ
 surrexérunt de sóliis suis,omnes
príncipes natiónum.

Univérsi respondébunt, et dicent tibi :
Et tu vulnerátus es sicut et
nos ; ecure   ecure   efféctus es.

Detrácta est ad ínferos supérbia tua,
 concídit   ecure   tuum ;subter te
sternétur tínea,et operiméntum tuum
erunt vermes.

Quómodo cecidísti de cælo,Lúcifer, qui
mane oriebáris ?corruísti in terram,
 qui vulnerábas gentes ?

 Qui dicébas in corde tuo :In cælum
conscéndam,super astra Deiexaltábo
sólium meum ;sedébo in monte
testaménti,in latéribus aquilónis ;

ascéndam super altitúdinem
núbium,   ecure   ero Altíssimo.
Verúmtamen ad inférnum detráheris,
 in profúndum laci

122

Luke 10:17-19 (English)

The seventy-two returned with joy and said, "Lord, even the demons submit to us in your name."

He replied, "I saw Satan fall like lightning from heaven. I have given you authority to trample on snakes and scorpions and to overcome all the power of the enemy; nothing will harm you.

Luke 10:17-19 (Latin)

Revérsi sunt autem septuagínta duo cum gáudio, dicéntes : Dómine, étiam dæmónia subjiciúntur nobis in   ecure   tuo.

Et ait illis : Vidébam Sátanam sicut fulgor de cælo cadéntem.
Ecce dedi vobis potestátem calcándi supra
   ecure o, et   ecure ou, et super omnem virtútem inimíci : et nihil vobis nocébit.

Note:

When reading group **A** Scriptures to instill faith, do so as if you are praying. Make the words real to you for you are reading cosmic principles that will strengthen you in your battle with the enemy.

When reading group **B** Scriptures to rebuke and establish dominance read them as commands. You are confirming eternal truths that deal directly with demonic or malevolent entities. When using these Scriptures you may have an incident of the unexplained phenomena or a sign that the Scriptures are having an effect. Many entities have a hatred of Scripture, especially the ones that envision their ultimate fate in hell.

So caution is needed, when you have their attention it is time to move onto commands.

Commands

As stated previously commands to entities are made from the general to the specific.

There are 4 types of commands that we shall examine here: claiming dominion, demanding attention, bindings and banishments.

Claiming Dominion: Using the authority of Christ you establish the ground rules of this encounter. Scripture says that Christ is, *"Far above all principality, and power, and might, and dominion, and every name that is named, not only in this world, but also in that which is to come"* **Ephesians 1:21 (KJV)**

Through Christ, you are in control of what goes on in the surroundings. The principalities, power and might that Scripture references as being demonic are made powerless through Christ, *"Blotting out the handwriting of ordinances that was against us, which was contrary to us, and took it out of the way, nailing it to his cross; And having spoiled principalities and powers, he made a shew of them openly, triumphing over them in it."* **Colossians 2:14-15 (KJV)**

Through the Cross and Jesus' death for our sins the powers of evil have no real power over us. The roles have been reversed, as being one with Christ we have authority over them.

Claiming dominion is stating this fact. It may have to be done many times if there is a response and a command forbidding interaction is ignored. Sometimes entities or demonic forces are stubborn. Whether it is a test of power or faith does not matter, determination and repetition may be required. Again, this is only if there is evidence that a challenge has been made by the entity.

Demanding Attention: Sometimes, like stubborn children various entities will pretend that they are oblivious to your commands. It allows them to linger in hopes that your faith may waver or in order to have you believe that they have gone.

Other times the entity will play a battle of wills with the Practitioner and the Associates. If there is a reason for the entity to stay, then the entity is strengthened and will resist. It could be a lack of faith or personal piety in respect to the Practitioner or the Associates, or the place itself might hold some lure or power for the entity.

Normally in cases of a blessing or consecration, there will be no need for more than one or two commands for attention. Again this depends upon any phenomena that might appear while performing the ceremonies.

Binding: This type of command would normally be used only once or twice in a blessing or consecration as well. It is to be used in conjunction with or shortly after claiming dominion. One purpose for this command is to prevent the entity from producing paranormal activity. Such activity can challenge faith by causing doubt or fear. Also it can prevent the entity from psychologically affecting any sensitive individuals on the team. It is to expressly restrain the entity from manifesting itself.

Binding also prevents the entity from communicating with any other spirits that might assist it in various fashions. Such assistance could be a transference or combining of power, causing confusion or distracting the team by manifesting itself with phenomena.

You can combine these binding commands as you see fit for the specific purposes you need in your encounters.

Banishment: This command is of course, self explanatory. You command the entity to leave the place and go to another specific area as discussed previously.

Claiming Dominion Commands

1) For the beginning of the ceremony

For Sovereign Control
We claim this (name area) in the name of the Lord Jesus Christ. God has put all things under Christ Jesus, be it dominions, powers, living and the dead. As a servant of Christ Jesus the Lord I now establish this (name area) is now under the Sovereign control of God the almighty.

Call for Obedience
All abiding in this place is under the power of Christ. All living, dead, spirit or any entity from this world or the next is under the dominion of the Creator, God Most High. And through His Only Begotten Son, Jesus Christ the Lord all here must submit to His authority. Through the blood of Christ and in the power of His Spirit, let all that dwell here obey.

Creator's Power over the Creation
All that is here is created. All that is here is from the Creator. There is nothing and no one that is not under His control. Through the name of the Lord Jesus Christ of Nazareth we establish that control on all that reside in this place. Through the Blood of Jesus you have no power. By the power of the Spirit of God you must obey.

God has Come, let Evil Beware
The Lord of the Universe has entered this place. Let all that oppose Him fear. The Only begotten Son of God is with us, let the oppressor beware. We come with the Word of God, the power of His Spirit and cleansed by the Blood of His only Son. Let every knee bow and tongue confess that Jesus Christ is Lord. Jesus Christ is Lord over this place.

Lord of Hosts
I come in the power of the Lord of Hosts and not my own. I come in the Name of the Lord Jesus Christ of Nazareth, the only begotten Son of God. And through the power of His Blood I proclaim His power, dominion and authority over all within this place.

Through the Servants of God
There is no power greater than God, no other cleaning but through the Blood of His only Son the Lord Jesus Christ. Through that Blood we come before all in this place and witness to the power of the Lord. Let those who have oppressed make no mistake, God is proclaiming His authority here through the mouths of His servants.

Through the Trinity (with Latin)
We proclaim that the Lord God reigns, let His creation tremble. We attest to the power of the Lord Jesus Christ and that all must listen. We claim this place through no authority of our own, but in the name of the Father, the Son and the Holy Spirit. Our God reigns in   ecure Patris, et Filii, et Spiritus Sancti. Amen.

2) At times of confrontation

Let the Enemy be Still
We reassert the power of Christ the Lord. Let the enemy be still. You have no right to resist; you are under the authority of the Lord Jesus Christ of Nazareth, only begotten Son of God. The Lord God reigns, let the earth be still.

Compelled to Obey
Under the power of Christ Jesus the Lord you are commanded to obey and be still. By being one with Christ through His shed blood and outpoured Spirit you have no other choice but to obey.

Awaiting Judgment
We resist you in the Name above all Names, the Lord of Hosts Christ Jesus the Lord. He is King of Kings and Lord of Lords, and we are His representatives through the shed Blood of the Cross. God has put all things in heaven, on Earth and Hades under His control. You are under His control and await your judgment. Your power was defeated at Calvary and you are compelled to obey.

Truth in the Face of Lies
Tricks, lies and deception are not truth. Jesus Christ is the Way, the Truth and the Life. No one comes to the Father except through Him. And we come through our Lord Jesus Christ and confront you with truth. We are more than conquerors through Him who loved us. You cannot come before the Father; and we, standing before Him command you to obey.

Triune Command

We rebuke you in the name of the Father, the Son and the Holy Spirit. By Yahweh the Creator through Jesus the Son and by the power of the Holy Spirit you are commanded to obey.

When Faith Waivers

We shall be still and know that God is with us. If God is with us, who can be against us? The Creator of the Cosmos gave His only begotten Son to dies for us so that we may have this victory over sin, death and evil. You have no power here.

Demanding Attention Commands

Power of the Blood

In Jesus Name through the power of His Blood you must obey.

Lord of Hosts

The Lord of Hosts commands you, the Lord Jesus Christ constraints you.

Abiding Power
You shall obey by the abiding power of the Father, the Son and the Holy Spirit.

Creator
Your Creator and Master abides in this place, you have no choice but to hearken and obey.

Still there
We know you are still here. You are commanded through the power of Jesus Christ of Nazareth, Lord of all, to obey.

King of Kings
It is not to you to choose, but to obey. The King of kings and Lord of lords commands you.

Not by Might
Not by might, not by power but by my Spirit says the Lord. The Lord commands you by His Spirit.

Creator Commands
As a creature, you are commanded to obey the Creator Whom we serve and through Who's Son, Jesus Christ of Nazareth, we serve.

Light of Glory
*In the Glory of the Lord nothing can be hidden.
We command you, spirit, to obey in the light of
the Lord Jesus Christ.*

Listen to Christ
*Jesus Christ the Son of God commands you to
listen to our words.*

Words of Power
*These words are truth, these words are power.
These are the words of Christ given through His
Spirit's power.*

Binding Commands

Binding by the Blood
*In the Name and in the power of the Lord Jesus
Christ we command all supernatural action
from any spirit in this building cease. The Lord
Jesus Christ commands you. We bind you by the
power of the Blood of Jesus Christ, only
begotten of God.*

Cutting of Power by the Blood

We bind any spirit residing in this place in the Blood of the Lord Jesus Christ. You are not allowed to manifest yourself in the physical world, kinetically or mentally. We cut off any alliances you have with the outside world with other entities in the power of the Lord of Hosts.

Triune Cleansing

We bind any unclean spirit from actively manifesting itself in this building. We plead the Blood of Christ over any connections to the occult, violent sin, or emotional turmoil. By the grace of God through Christ we severe all such connections and bind any entity thriving on such, in the name of the Father, Son and Holy Spirit.

Petition for Cessation

Lord Jesus Christ, we come before you and ask that you would bind the power of any entity in this (location). As Lord of hosts you command the living and the dead; whatever type of entity we encounter here has to obey. We ask it in Your Name, Jesus Christ, only begotten of the Father. Whatever abides here, you are forbidden to manifest yourself or seek influence or power. The Spirit of God constrains you.

135

Christ the Righteous

In the name of the Holy One, King of kings, Lord of lords, Jesus Christ the righteous, we invoke the Lordship of Christ over this place. Any spirit abiding here may not manifest power to harm or influence anyone here and we cut off any familiar spirits that might give aid.

Lord of the Hosts of Heaven

Jesus Christ of Nazareth, Lord of Hosts, we call upon the host of heaven, the messengers of the Lord Most High to aid us and form a circle of defense around this place. We call upon the angels of God to aid us as we in the Name of Christ our Lord cut off this spirit from all outside strength, power and dominion. We call upon the faithful to help us in our battle with the fallen and tie the hand of any power that lingers here.

Christ Abides

The Lord Jesus Christ is in this place, as two or three gather. The power of Christ is in this place as prayers are answered. The love of Christ abides in this place as sins are forgiven. The vengeance and dominion of the kingdom of Christ is exalted and let all evil know the Lord of Hosts has entered in. Your power is neutered and your influence overthrown.

Cleansing and Dominion

Jesus Christ was given all authority over heaven and earth, and we as those who call on His name and are washed in his precious blood come here today in that authority. We cut off the dominion in this place of any unclean spirit, in the Name of the Lord Jesus Christ. We ask forgiveness and cleansing for any act or disobedience that was perpetrated or contrived in this place that might give the enemy power or excuse for influence here. In the forgiveness of His Word and the washing of His Blood we claim this place for Christ Jesus the Lord and claim His dominion here. Anything that dwells here cannot influence, harass or manifest themselves in anyway, we testify in the Name of Jesus Christ the Lord of Hosts.

Reclaiming the Territory

As the power of the Cross of Christ Jesus made it possible for all to be free, the precious Blood that flowed from that Cross broke all power and control by any entity, spirit or being over any person who claims cleansing in the Blood of the Lord Jesus Christ. And in the Name of Christ the Lord we claim this place for Christ and plead the Blood over it. All things bound to evil or occult are hereby broken in the name of the Lord Jesus Christ and by the assent of the owner of this place.

137

Owners Consent

As (name of owner) has repented and severed all ties to (name of offense) and has asked forgiveness in the Blood of Christ, we come now to through that cleansing to re-establish the rule of Christ in this place. Sin has been forgiven; ties to sin and evil have been broken through the grace of our Lord Jesus Christ. We claim the victory Jesus won on the Cross and sever the power of the enemy in this place.

Power over Compulsion

We sever the power that compulsive sin had over this place and by the Blood of Christ, we reclaim it through the Grace of The Lord Jesus brought through the Cross.

Procession of Power

We sever the ties of sin in the Blood of Christ, we sever the curse of the past in the Grace of God. We defeat the power of trauma through the love of Jesus Christ, we oppose the power of oppression through the victory of the Cross. All links to evil have been torn asunder by the gift of God's Son at Calvary through His atoning Blood. All power of the enemy here has been rendered useless when faced by the power of an awesome God, who we represent, through Jesus Christ the Lord. All entities here are bound through Christ, rendered powerless by the Cross.

Banishment Commands

Just Leave

In the Name of the Lord Jesus Christ, Lord of the living and the dead, we command you to leave this place and never to return. This place is not yours to inhabit, it belongs to (name the owners). We command you go to leave and never return.

Go to the Pit

In the Name of Jesus Christ our Lord, we command you spirit to leave this place and to never return. We command you to go to the pit and await the fate which God has in store for you on the last day.

Variable Triune

Be it that we claim this place in the Name of the Father, the Son and the Holy Spirit (use holy water if you wish, on the utterance of each name sprinkled around you), we command you by the power of the Lord of Hosts to leave this place. We cast you out into (use any of these as appropriate: the wilderness, the pit, Sheol, Hades) where you can bother these people no more.

Old Style Banishment

We call upon the Spirit of God to come in and drive you out, O foul spirit. We command you to go into the abyss where you can bother no one else hence forth. We command you to flee in the name of the Lord Jesus Christ and through the power of His name.

Continuative

Having been bound through the power of the redemptive Blood of Jesus Christ shed on the Cross we consign you once again unclean spirit to fester once more in the pit, awaiting the fate God has in store with you, the Devil and all the minions of iniquity. We cast you thus into the pit through the power of Christ Jesus the Lord

To Sheol

The Lord Jesus Christ, having triumphed over all principalities, powers and dominions through the Blood of the Cross, now sits at the right hand of God the Father. Through The Name of that selfsame Jesus Christ of Nazareth we command you now spirit to depart this place and be bound in Sheol, where the dead await the final judgment. This we command in the Name of the Father, the Son and the Holy Spirit.

Into the Wilderness

We command any spirit dwelling here to obey the Lord Jesus Christ. You are no longer allowed to be here. You have no right to be here. All connections have been severed for you. And the owners wish you be gone. So in the Name of the Lord Jesus Christ we command you to leave this place and go into the wilderness where you will find no satisfaction to quench your thirst. Through the authority of Christ Jesus we command you, leave now!

By the Authority of Christ

All authority and dominion belong to our Lord and Savior Jesus Christ, only begotten Son of God. Through Christ's Name we now call upon all spirits of fear and dread to leave this place. Through Christ's Name all spirits of despair and oppression leave this place. Through Christ's Name all unclean minions of evil, unseen workers of darkness leave this place. We cast you into the abyss that has no end where you await judgment. Leave this place to never return.

Legal Dominion over Unknown Entity

By the authority vested in me by the cleansing Blood of Jesus Christ we command all spirits leave this place. This is no longer your dwelling place, it belongs to the living sons of men. We cast you out commanding you go to the grave, and wait in Sheol until the final judgment. Not by our own might, power or authority do we demand this, but through the power of the Risen Lord Jesus Christ the Righteous.

Old Rhyme Command

The bonds were broke,
let the powers be shattered
God has spoke,
Let His enemies be scattered.
Through the Cross is the final defeat,
All His enemies lay crushed at His feet.
Awake and away, evil ones you must flee,
To the pit of judgment where fate awaits thee.
Through Christ the Lord, in His name we pray,
We cast you out spirit, to be bound till the last day.

Consecration Closings

Offering to God

Unto you Oh God do we lift up this place.

We offer it to you as a clean vessel in which we ask you to abide

We plead the Blood of the Lord Jesus Christ over the building and ask you to forgive all generational curses, sins or abominations.

We ask your Holy Spirit's presence to dwell here and make this a place of peace where the only presence felt is the comforting love of Thy Holy Ghost.

Bless all those who come in and go out and may Your love and comfort be an ever present assurance of Your care.

We surrender all ownership of this place and dedicate this place unto You, O God.

We give this place now to You as Your dwelling place and we ask your angels to guard it. Amen.

Thanks and Giving

Lord God, we thank you for the love you showed to us on Calvary.

We thank you for the precious Blood of the Lord Jesus Christ that washes us clean from all sin and that has given us the victory this day.

As we come before You, Lord of Hosts, we offer up this place unto You and ask that you would sanctify it by Thy Blood.

As an empty vessel fill it with the presence of thy Holy Spirit. Purge out any lingering uncleanness.

We ask that You would bless this place and all that dwell therein.

Guard it and keep it as a Holy place dedicated unto You. We ask, Lord of Hosts that You would set Your angels as guardians around and about this place.

We pray you would not stand for any evil being to enter this place, and we pray Your divine protection as we dedicate it to You. Amen.

Praise Dedication

Lord we thank You for the Victory we have received by Your Grace.

Thank You Lord Jesus Christ, Savior and Coming King for your ever present power and assurance of faith that You always give us.

We affirm our love for You O Lord, and Praise Your Holy Name. We ask that Your sweet presence will fill this place that was once ruled by fear and dread.

May those who dwell herein find here nothing but peace, comfort and assurance of Your mighty presence as You guard and protect them with Your love, and forgive them daily by the washing away of sin by the power of the Cross.

Thank you Abba Father that we are more than conquerors through Him who loved us and we now surrender this place unto you and ask that you would bless it and keep it to the Glory of Your Holy Name.

Amen.

Prayer of Keeping

We claim this place in the Name of the Father, the Son and the Holy Spirit. (You may sprinkle Holy Water at each name)

We now dedicate this place to the service of the Lord Jesus Christ, only begotten Son of the Most High God.

Lord, we ask You loving presence be ever felt here, Holy Spirit we invite you to dwell here, fill every room, every corner and every hidden place with Your healing grace.

Father God we ask You would keep a watchful eye over this (household or name of place) and keep all who dwell within in Your graces.

We set a barrier around this house, a barrier of prayer and grace through the power of the triune God that no evil may come back here. We ask the presence of your guardian angels O Lord to stand guard and resist any spirit that might try to return.

In Jesus Name we pray, Amen.

A Gaelic Blessing

Dia, cosain seo gnáth gnách.
Go raibh maith agat Dia , Tá tú mo
foscadh.
Is dubhar thu ri teas,
Is seasgar thu ri fuachd,
Is suilean thu dha'n dall,
Is crann dh' an deoraidh thruagh,
Is eilean thu air muir,
Is cuisil thu air tir,
Is fuaran thu am fasach,
Is slaint dha'n   ecure tinn.
Thainig's Iosa Criosda ciuin,
Thainig's Spiorad fior an iuil.
Thainig's Righ nan righ air stiuir,
Tri Naomh na Gloire
Bhith 'n comhnuidh rium reidh,
Ri m' eachraidh, ri m' lochraidh,
Ri cioba cloimh an treud.
Am barr ta fas air raona
No caonachadh an raoid,
Air machair no air mointeach,
An toit, an torr, no an cruach.
Gach ni tha'n aird no'n iosal,
Gach insridh agus buar,
'S le Trithinn naomh na gloire,
oir is leatsa an rìoghachd,
agus an cumhachd,
agus a' glòir,
gu sìorraidh. Amen

A Gaelic Blessings (English)
God, protect this place.
Thank you God, You are my shelter.
A shade art thou in the heat,
A shelter art thou in the cold,
Eyes art thou to the blind,
A staff art thou to the pilgrim,
An island art thou at sea,
A fortress art thou on land,
A well art thou in the desert,
Health art thou to the ailing.
Jesus Christ has come,
And the Spirit of true guidance has
come,
And the King of kings has come on the
helm,
Be the sacred Three of Glory
Aye at peace with me,
With my horses, with my cattle,
With my woolly sheep in flocks.
With the crops growing in the field
Or ripening in the sheaf,
On the machair, on the moor,
In cole, in heap, or stack.
Every thing on high or low,
Every furnishing and flock,
Belong to the holy Triune of glory
For thine is the kingdom,
and the power, and the glory,
for ever. Amen.

Latin Prayer of Dedication

Actiones nostras, quaesumus Domine,
aspirando praeveni et adiuvando
prosequere: ut cuncta nosta oratio et
operatio a te   ecure incipiat et per ta
coepta finiatur.

Da, Domine,   ecure   ous pacem in
diebus nostis, ut, ope misericordiae tuae
adiuti, et a peccato simus   ecure liberi
et ab omni perturbatione   ecure.

Veni, Sancte Spiritus, reple tuorum
aedificium fidelium, et tui amoris in eis
ignem accende.

Suscipe, Domine, universam meam
libertatem. Accipe memoriam,
intellectum atque voluntatem omnem.
Quidquid habeo vel possideo mihi
largitus es; id tibi totum restituo, ac tuae
prorsus voluntati trado gubernandum.
Amorem tui solum cum gratia tua mihi
dones, et dives sum satis, nec aliud
quidquam ultra posco. Amen

Latin Prayer of Dedication (English)
Go before us, O Lord, we beseech Thee,
in all our doings with Thy gracious
inspiration, and further us with Thy
continual help, that every prayer and
work of ours may begin from Thee, and
by Thee be duly ended.

Graciously give peace, O Lord, in our
days, that, being assisted by help of Thy
mercy, we may ever be free from sin
and safe from all disturbance.

Come, Holy Spirit, fill the building of
Thy faithful and kindle in them the fire
of Thy love.

Lord Jesus Christ, take all my freedom,
my memory, my understanding, and my
will. All that I have and cherish Thou
hast given me. I surrender it all to be
guided by Thy will. Thy grace and Thy
love are wealth enough for me. Give me
these Lord Jesus and I ask for nothing
more. Amen.

Considerations
And Conclusion

Again, the format to use the preceding material can vary to accomade the particular situation you are confronted with. The basic outline of this system is:

Preperation
Sealing
Binding
Casting
Consecration

Keep in mind the Binding and Casting are commands, so are in the Commands Chapter.

In using the prayers, commands and Scriptures in the previous chapters, here are a few examples; where there is both English and other language versions you may use your discretion so long as if the others in your company know the meaning of the prayer or Scripture:

For a basic ceremony after a reported entity (non hostile)

Preperation
Prayer of Cleansing and Empowerment p39
Romans 8:38-39 p76

Sealing
Power of the Name Prayer with Holy Water p65

Binding
Christ the Righteous p136
Psalm 44:4-8, 25-26 Pp79-80

Casting
Variable Triune p139

Consecration
Prayer of Keeping p126
Guardina Angel Prayer p40

Basic ceremony after a reported hostile entity
encounter:

Preperation
Prayer of Empowerment p42
Ephesians 6:10-18 Pp74-75
For Soviergn Control p128

Sealing
General Sealing Prayer 2 p64
Colossians 2:13-15 p111

Binding
Triune Cleansing p135

Casting
By the Authority of Christ p141

Consecration
Thanks and Giving p144

If there is manifestations of phenomena during the ritual use demanding attention or claiming dominion commands until it dissipates. Use your own descrection

Reasons why the ceremony may not work

1) Occult Ties

If there is any involvement in the occult by the owners or residents of the place being blessed, it needs to come into the forefront before the intervention begins. Otherwise the process will be a fruitless and involved affair which may harm the client, associates and even the practitioner.

Many times the client may not divulge any occult associations because of guilt, sin or even demonic manipulation. Often it is a teenage family member whose ties to the occult have not been made known to the family at large as of the time of the ceremony.

A honest and forthright interview needs to be given prior to the ceremony. Often times the practitioner or associate who is gifted with the Spiritual Gift of Discernment of Spirits may have a sense that there are occult forces at work in the location and the interview needs to be pointed and blunt. Many times the resident or owner might not even think of the practice that they have been engaged in is in its basic nature an occult association. There are times when the practice that harbors occult focus or power might be an innocent thing in and of itself. Likewise there can be seemingly occult practices made by the owner or resident that have no occult power or entanglements.

If there is an occult connection, the one who has been doing these practices needs to verbally renounce these practices in front of others and make a serious attempt at repentance. Otherwise the ceremony should not take place. It may often be that the investigation into the incident will bring about occult activity that the resident or owner does not want to give up. The practitioner and associates should not pressure the person to relinquish the occult ties. Frank and pointed language as to the nature of these ties should be given, and the need for the person or persons to severe all such bonds. However, it is essential that there is no manipulation by the practitioner or associates in regard to the repentance. It needs to be heartfelt and sincere, or the person who you wish to help may end up in worse condition than they were before your intercession.

Once again Jesus told us in **Luke 11:24-26**,

"When the unclean spirit is gone out of a man, he walketh through dry places, seeking rest; and finding none, he saith, I will return unto my house whence I came out.

And when he cometh, he findeth it swept and garnished.

Then goeth he, and taketh to him seven other spirits more wicked than himself; and they enter in, and dwell there: and the last state of that man is worse than the first."

I will not make a list here of Occult practices, to find such I would recommend 'Occult A B C' by Kurt Koch for a very inclusive and stringent list.

However once again I would like to reiterate that some things may have occult appearance and not ties or power therin and likewise the most innocent of things could have an occult or demonic tie.

The psychiatrist can use a pendulum to have the patient reach inside himself and find his true feelings, leading to a breakthrough. For the psychiatrist knows that the mind and minute muscle reflexes are what makes the pendulum swing to and from in predictable patterns.

Whereas the medium uses the pendulum to interact with a spirit. That person believes they are interacting with a spirit, and even if they initially are not, it can draw a demonic presence who will respond to the mediums questions.

2) **Generational Issues**

The second Commandment given by God to Moses as related in **Exodus 20:4-6** says: *"Thou shalt not make unto thee any graven image, or any likeness of any thing that is in heaven above, or that is in the earth beneath, or that is in the water under the earth. Thou shalt not bow down thyself to them, nor serve them: for I the LORD thy God am a jealous God, visiting the iniquity of the fathers upon the children unto the third and fourth generation of them that hate me; And shewing mercy unto thousands of them that love me, and keep my commandments."*

Sin and occult associations are passed down spiritually from generation to generation unless there is a break in the chain. Now it does not seem fair, an innocent grandchild may suffer from the actions of their grandfather or grandmother. But as we know in psychological issues such as co-dependency that patterns of behavior can echo down from one generation to another. In the end the issues of addicition or behavior may differ significantly from the point of origin in an ancestor, but nevertheless the negative and destructive habitual patterns remain the same.

These psychological principles hold true for the spiritual as well.

A grandfather is involved deeply with the occult. He has familiar spirits that help him in divination or magical ritual. They visit the family from generation to generation in various incarnations. From fortune telling to depression or paranormal phenomena, the grandfathers dabbling in the dark is manifest in his offspring. Only by a renunciation, repentance and commitment to Christ can break such bonds, be it by sin or the occult.

Sexual or violent assaults can also manifest spiritually and pass from generations both psychologically and spiritually as well. Once again the end results might not look like the origin of the oppression.

The practitioner and the associates need to dig deep into family history to uncover any such issues that may be manifesting in the present.

Psychological issues such as depression, multiple personalities,and personality disorders may be simply conditional and psychological. Then again they may be symptoms of a generational spiritual issue. Caution, tact and an open mind are of the utmost importance when it comes to such issues. Usually if the person manifests such psychological problems and clinical help and medication are not working efficiently there could be a spiritual link. But never, I repeat, never assume a psychological problem has a spiritual root. Clients with spiritual issues that manifest themselves psychologically almost always have other issues involved as well. If you observe disturbing behavior and the person is not seeking treatment, it is advisable that you tactfully let the client know that before you can help them they need to seek medical attention. It is not an easy thing to do tactfully, you may have to just turn down the assignment and let a loved one know of your concerns. However I would advise against thepreforming of the ceremony is there are unresolved issues of any kind.

3) An Extreemly Powerful Entity

Mark 9:17-29 tells of a possessed man whom the Disciples could not exorcise the foul spirit from,

"And one of the multitude answered and said, Master, I have brought unto thee my son, which hath a dumb spirit; And wheresoever he taketh him, he teareth him: and he foameth, and gnasheth with his teeth, and pineth away: and I spake to thy disciples that they should cast him out; and they could not. He answereth him, and saith, O faithless generation, how long shall I be with you? how long shall I suffer you? bring him unto me. And they brought him unto him: and when he saw him, straightway the spirit tare him; and he fell on the ground, and wallowed foaming. And he asked his father, How long is it ago since this came unto him? And he said, Of a child. And ofttimes it hath cast him into the fire, and into the waters, to destroy him: but if thou canst do any thing, have compassion on us, and help us. Jesus said unto him, If thou canst believe, all things are possible to him that believeth. And straightway the father of the child cried out, and said with tears, Lord, I believe; help thou mine unbelief. When Jesus saw that the people came running together, he rebuked the foul spirit, saying unto him, Thou dumb and deaf spirit, I charge thee, come out of him, and enter no more into him. And the spirit cried, and rent him sore, and came out of him: and he was as one dead; insomuch that many said, He is dead. But Jesus took him by the hand, and lifted him up; and he arose. And when he

was come into the house, his disciples asked him privately, Why could not we cast him out? And he said unto them, This kind can come forth by nothing, but by prayer and fasting."

Some entities are stronger than others. Although the example set forth here from Scripture is that of a possession of a human being the same principle applies to blessings and consecration whee entities are involved. There needs to be some extra effort extended for the extrication of the entity. Fasting mized with prayer heightens the spiritual awareness. Fasting has long been a means to not only clean the body from imputiries but a means of spiritual clarity.

Chemical reactions within the body bring a heightened state of awareness that are conductive with spirituality. Regularly fasting is done in private and without the knowledge of others. However, with fasting and prayer because of a power encounter with an entity it is necessary to have corperate fasting and prayer between the practitioner and the associates.

The length that the group needs to be in fasting and prayer is up to the individual, but a predestined time frame should be followed unless of physical inability. Also if the practitioner or any of the associates have a

160

medical issue such as diabetes limited fasting should be observed. Limited fasting is selecting foods to avoid or limiting oneself to one specific food, depending on the medical necessity. While the fasting my last a day or more, there should be times of corperate prayer where the group focuses on praise to the Lord and intercession for the people involved with the ceremony. Praise is a primary ingredient in spiritual warfare, and while intercession and rebuking of the entity is necessary, it should not be the focus. The Lord is the One who is wins the battle, we are mearly vessels for His grace and power. In the above Scripture the disciples could not exorcise the demon from the tormented boy and all Jesus had to do was issue a simple command. Likewise we must ever be aware that without the Lord we can do nothing. That is the reason for the necessity of fasting, to have us draw near with aheart transformed by faith as an assistance for our unbelief.

4) Disbelief or Lack of Faith

One does not need to be ashamed if they have a crisis of faith, especially when it comes to spiritual warfare. Saints of great faith have had their times of doubt as well. It is said that in her later years, Mother Teresa had a serious crisis of faith, being racked with doubt and feeling like a complete failure.

Doubt merely means we are human. Even Jesus Himself on the Cross had a moment of human doubt prophesized in Old Testament Scripture. **Matthew 27:45-46** tells us: *"Now from the sixth hour there was darkness over all the land unto the ninth hour. And about the ninth hour Jesus cried with a loud voice, saying, Eli, Eli, lama sabachthani? that is to say, My God, my God, why hast thou forsaken me?"* Christ quotes **Psalm 22:1** at the moment that God put all the sin of eternity on His only Son and looked away. Although as fully God, Christ knew what was to transpire, as fully man His heart sank.

The possibility of lack of or wavering faith is why the practitioner needs a solid team of associates and prayer backup. If one link in the chain fails, the others can uplift the weakening link. The team works together to encourage and support one another, an effective weapon in the Lord's hand.

There could also be the possibility of wavering or lack of faith with the owner or resident. This also needs to be addressed. Counseling and reassurance prior to the ceremony should be aimed at alieving any fears the owner or resident has that the ritual will not work. Of course with a third party there is never a guarantee that the person will have faith at all, so knowing your client is essential when assessing the situation.

5) **Sin**

As stated in the opening chapter, if there is unconfessed sin with the practitioner or any associate you run the risk of all your efforts being for naught. Once again, I must reiterate, keep a short account with God.

Use of Holy Water and Incense

Throughout this ceremony you may feel free to use incense or Holy Water. There are specific prayers and commands where I noted the use of them, but they are not limited to those areas.

When using Holy Water it is a traditional exercise to invoke the triune name of the Trinity. While it is not necessary, I find it very usefull since it is an age old tradition, and entities know the tradition very well. It is, in effect, a doubly whammy.

Incense is used as a symbol of the prayers of God's people. As the smoke from the incense rises up to the sky, so do our prayers acend into heaven. In the Book of the Revelation we see this typology as St. John gives us a window to heaven in the last days: *"And when he had opened the seventh seal, there was silence in heaven about the space of half an hour. And I saw the seven angels which stood before God; and to them were given seven trumpets. And another angel came and stood at the altar, having a golden censer; and there was given unto him much incense, that he should offer it with the prayers of all saints upon the golden altar which was before the throne. And the smoke of the incense, which came with the prayers of the saints, ascended up before God out of the angel's hand."* **Revelation 8:1-4.** Therefore incense combined with prayer gives a vivid representation of our prayers ascending to the ear of God.

In Conclusion:

I pray that this brief guide may help you as you help others find peace. It is by no means a comprehensive guide, and it reflects only one branch of Christian practice on the subject. Feel free to use your own prayers and research more into church history or your own faith traditions to further tailor the ceremony to your needs.

Please remember, in the area of demonology, there are no experts. Scripture is very aloof when it comes to the nature and persona of spirits and entities. We rely on church tradition and conjecture. Even those with Seminary training on the subject such as mysel are but neophytes. We know what these beings are not, but we do not precisely know what they are.

Once again this is a ritual for everyone of faith. There are dangers if you use the ceremony here without a deep faith background and a strong relationship with the Lord. You could end up oppressed yourself or worse. So use this guide with faith, caution and the reliance on others of deep faith.

In closing I would like to include the Ritual Romanum, the only formal exorcism rite sanctioned by the Roman catholic Church. It originated in the Roman Church in 1614 during the time of Pope Paul V. While we are not dealing here in this guide with demonic possession, it offers us a look into a version of the rite from which this ceremony is historically derived.

The Ritual Romanum

I exorcise you, most vile spirit, the very
incarnation of our adversary, the specter, the
enemy, in the name of Jesus Christ to get out
and flee from this creature of God. He himself
commands you who ordered you thrown from
the heights of heaven to the dpths of the earth.
He commands you, who rules the sea, the winds
and tempests. Hear, therefore and shudder, O
Satan, you enemy of the human race, cause of
death, thief of life, destroyer of justice, source
of evils, root of vice, seducer of men, betrayer
of natins, source of jealousy, origin of avarice,
cause of discord, procurer of sorrows-why do
you remain and resist when you know that Jesus
Christ blocks your plans? Fear him who in Isaac
was immolated, who was sold in Joseph, who
was killed in the lamb, who was crucified in the
man and then became the conqueror of hell...

Most vile dragon, in the name of the immaculate
lam, who trod upon the asp and the basilisk,
who conquered the lion and dragon, I command
you to get out of this man, to get out of the
Church of God. Tremble and flee at the name
which Hell fears; that name to which the virtues
of heaven, the powers and the dominions are
subject, which the cherubim and seraphim
praise with untiring voices, chanting, Holy,
Holy, Holy, Lord of the Sabaoth.

Christian Home Blessing Kit

Includes a Christian Mezuzah, incense censur, blessed incense, Holy Water and blessing guide. Cost: $20.00

Christian Mezuzah

Made with Holy Water with Greek and Hebrew Scripture encircling, and a cross and scroll in the center with the Scripture **Romans 8:23-28**. Cost $10.00

E-mail **Opengate@roadrunner.com** for details